CONTENTS

Introduction: Discover New England! **5**
*All the charm of the Founders' Period far removed from
the American way of life*

History at a glance **6**

New England in context: From architecture to puritanism **11**
*New England cultivates its own – Old English – style, one which
attracts tourists, the most enduring source of income, like magic*

Food & drink: Lobster galore **17**
*New England's lobsters are famous. Lobster arrives on the table in
every imaginable variation*

Shopping & souvenirs: Folklore, collectibles and outlet shopping **19**
*Typically New England: useful things and old stuff attract the
souvenir hunter*

Events: Pride in history and tradition **21**
*New England celebrates Washington's Birthday just as majestically
as a rowing contest at the elite schools*

Connecticut and Rhode Island: Water, wind and untamed forests **25**
*In Connecticut and Rhode Island travellers find a striking contrast:
a sense of timelessness along with well-to-do residents*

Massachusetts: Pace setter in the northeast **39**
*In the centre of New England: beaches, winter sports
and old fishing ports*

Vermont and New Hampshire: Solitary life and love of freedom **61**
*Each year autumn is ablaze in New England's
mountainous north*

Maine: The land of lighthouses and seclusion **75**
*A rugged sea coast, islands, mountains, clear rivers and lakes have
lured summer holiday makers for generations*

Long Island: Playground for New York's society **85**
*Long Island: empty beaches, soft breakers and a breath
of exclusivity*

Routes in New England **93**

Essentials: Practical information **97**

Do's and don'ts **102**

Road Atlas of New England **103**

Index **111**

What do you get for your money? **112**

Discover New England!

All the charm of the Founders' Period far removed from the American way of life

Among the many characteristics of America one finds only few – 500 years after the continent's discovery by Christopher Columbus – in which remnants of European cultural tradition have survived. The land of unlimited possibilities has all but cut itself free from the European motherland.

That is certainly also valid for New England, the stretch of continent in the furthest northeastern reaches of the US. And yet, amazingly, it is there, where the country associated with comics, cowboys and computers once began. Small and unassuming, the flair of the "Founding Fathers", with their Old English style, can still be found. Among the jutting, sandy bays of Cape Cod and the rugged cliffs of Maine, the far and secluded wooded heights of Vermont and the hustle and bustle of Boston, Old England survives. Those interested in the

Wooden houses, an old tradition that is deceptive: time doesn't actually stand still in New England

"New World" will be immediately fascinated by the manner in which the culture of Old England stoically continues going its own way.

The tiny corner tucked into America's northeast, despite its small size, is much more than a symbol or some sort of tourist attraction.

New England is the heartland of the original 13 states that broke free of the British Crown in 1776 and in a long and bitter war won their independence to establish the world's first democracy since the Classical Age. This region has helped to determine each and every phase of American development from the time it was a colony of exiled people to its present status as the pre-eminent nation of today.

That all would never have been realizable had New England not established one of the most outstanding university systems in the world early on elite universities such as Harvard and Yale contributed to the expedition of America's transition from agriculture and fishing to industrialized nation. It was in

History at a glance

1000
Leif Ericson and the Vikings sail to Maine

1604
Samuel de Champlain explores America's Northeast

1614
New England claimed by the British Crown

1620
Arrival of the pilgrims on the "Mayflower" in Plymouth

1630
Boston is founded, followed by Hartford (1635), Providence (1636) and Portsmouth (1638)

1635
Harvard University opens

1752
The number of inhabitants in Boston totals 50,000

1765
The attempt to tax colonists with the Stamp Act leads to the *Boston Massacre* (1770) and *Boston Tea Party* (1773), milestones on the road to independence

1776
The American colonies declare their independence from Great Britain

1789
Head of the Armed Forces, George Washington becomes the first president of the United States

1791
Vermont joins the Union as 14th state

1820
Maine becomes the 23rd state

1845
Famine at home brings thousands of Irish to New England

1850
Highpoint of whaling and the heyday of overseas trade; industrialisation creates metalworking enterprises, spinning and weaving mills and harves

1854
Opening of the Boston Public Library, the first library in the world open to everyone

1865
With the Union's victory in the Civil War (begun in 1961), the northern states are finally able to abolish slavery in the US

1900
The end of Puritan dominance. The majority of New England politicians are Catholics

1954
Launching of the *Nautilus*, the world's first atomic submarine, in Groton/Connecticut

1960
Senator John F. Kennedy, a Boston native, becomes the first catholic U.S. President

1992
Indians in southeastern Connecticut build Foxwoods, most profitable gambling casino in the world – becoming millionaires

Connecticut and Massachusetts that the stage coaches and revolvers were produced with which the wild west was tamed and "Manifest Destiny" realized. It was in Hartford, not in Detroit, where the first autos rolled off the assembly line, putting America on wheels. The textile spinning mills in New Hampshire and Rhode Island spun the yarn to clothe the nation; those states also launched the atomic submarines which finally tilted the frightening balance with the Soviets in the Cold War in favour of the west.

Trappers and farmers, inventors and industrialists, teachers and professors, priests and poets are an invisible but enduring coalition. Their renowned accomplishment being that of cultivating the land, not exploiting it.

Granted, much of this has become history. And while the US continues to grow and grow with no limits in sight, New England slowly drifts to the rim. The real powerhouse of America is to be found today in that "sun belt" stretching from California over Arizona out to Texas and Florida. The one-time energy centre gives the impression that in those spic-and-span towns you find that time there has simply stood still. Yet appearances are deceiving. And just as the Puritan Ethic of New England armed with its conservative basic values and unbridled free enterprise spirit still subliminally determines the day-to-day course of affairs, respect for tradition and a healthy sense of proportion with regard to the ecology have also become weighty factors in modern consciousness. Needless to say, in New England this is nothing new and New Englanders are well ahead of their time.

It may simply be a matter of New England being among the first states to have found its way to an identity. New England, in the opinion of the writer Bernard De Vito as expressed in the 1930s, must avoid the temptation to grow and must avoid "change for the mere sake of change". New England is America – complete and perfect. Here people still build houses out of wood, and they prefer the style of previous times. Tolerance in political discussion is still the norm and a good deal of effort is expended on maintaining and extending museums, concert halls and theatres. Viewed as "the country" and as such the traditional recreation area of rich city people from Boston and New York (itself, incidentally not considered part of New England!) this region, aside from a few minor outcroppings of shopping malls and motel strips, has never sacrificed its original character. The money from holidaymakers and house owners, combined with their own interest in maintaining an intact little world, have infused new economic life into many spots in a healthy more than harmful way.

The towns which stretch along the coast from Greenwich in Connecticut to Bangor in Maine possess a rich history. Overseas trade and whaling financed the earlier prosperity here. Nowadays those piers, warehouses and streets found along the Atlantic are well tended restaurants and shops.

The picture of New England which instantly comes to mind

is one of tiny villages with white picket fences set out in the country, planned and laid out by the original settlers with splendid wooden churches, stately residences, a general store, a town hall and a central greenbelt, i.e. a parklike area with lawns and shady trees in the middle.

The charm of these places, which seem to carry on the Old English tradition as if it were the most natural thing in the world, is all the more enhanced when maple, birch, oak and hickory, with their colourful autumn leaves unfurl a panorama of colour which recalls the war-paint of yesteryear.

The woods, which cover more than 70 per cent of the entire area, were not planted by human hand but rather "grew themselves" everywhere, causing farmers to abandon the farmland for economic reasons and travel westward more than a hundred years ago. Old growth forests left undisturbed allow the spectacular yellows and reds of autumn to blaze across the landscape.

The seasons also alter the appearance of the landscape itself. The bare winter vegetation is overwhelmed by a green as thick as a jungle the moment the temperature rises to remain a stable 20°C (68°F). The sticky-warm summers lure bathing enthusiasts to the traditional swimming areas on the ocean while hikers, cyclists and rapids-riskers are drawn to the less muggy highland to elevations of 1,000 metres and more. It starts to become chilly along the coast in the early autumn and the fishing villages become cool and quiet. If it weren't for the skiers and cross-country fans, New England would drift off into a Rip-Van-Winkel slumber lasting all through the long winter.

The winters here are long and hard, which is the reason why agriculture, aside from the luscious fruit- and vegetable farms in Connecticut's warmer climes and the extensive potato cultivation in the rural areas of Maine are limited chiefly to milk production and poultry breeding.

In 1614 a British captain, along with the Pilgrim Fathers, christened the New World with the landing of the "Mayflower" as they begun the arduous American adventure of settling the New World. Today 13 million people live in the six federal states of Connecticut, Maine, Massachusetts, New Hampshire, Rhode Island and Vermont. Among them are also to be found those few who see in themselves the only true Yankees. For these select, the word, derived from the Dutch and (in)famous the world over, is not a term of reproach, but one of merit. The Yankees represent and cherish the traditional values: diligence, discipline, modesty and the ability to make the best out of every situation. Meanwhile, of course, the ancestors of immigrants from Ireland, Italy, French-speaking Canada, Scandinavia and Jews from Eastern Europe are also proud of their Yankeeness. Yet an exact understanding of just what Yankeedom means changes from states to state and is recognisable by its nuances. For instance for the Connecticut Yankees, a good, healthy business sense is paramount. And while New Hampshire Yankees have the ill-fame of being stingy and reserved, it certainly doesn't keep them from welcoming tourists with open arms. Maine Yankees, it is said, never utter one single word more than is absolutely necessary and have even become a bit quirky in the isolation and remoteness; but then among Massachusetts Yankees, education, political involvement and class consciousness are high on the scale of values.

Whoever travels to New England may understandably be somewhat less interested in all this all at once, especially if the traveller happens to be searching above all for peace and quiet, a rough, northern climate, empty beaches, fresh lobster and clams and the colourful glory of autumn's leaves.

Likewise the inclination so common among Americans to cultivate their own history may not win such wide acceptance among foreign (or domestic!) travellers. But sooner or later everyone feels that without the people who live here with their good New England spirit, without the realisation that wood is more elegant than plastic, that a certain reserve is more becoming than a sales pitch, long-term profits better than a "fast buck", all the nature in the world would be nothing more than some Disneyland transported northwards. But for New England itself, often called "America's attic".

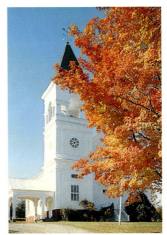

Typical for New England: wooden architecture and Indian Summer

The landscape was created by ice masses of previous millennia. The heights of the White and Green Mountains, the Taconites and Monadnocks tower over a region which is cut from north to south into two unequal halves by the 600-km-long Connecticut River and is decorated in spectacular fashion by wild cliffs along the coast, which streches for thousands of kilometres.

The landscape makes New England an ideal tourist destination for those on the lookout for untouched nature as well as a multitude of differing sights. The traveller experiences a world, in all its antiquated beauty, from which the entire continent was once conquered. A visit to New England is more than a trip to just another country or just another state. It is a trip to another time, one which, happily, is not yet past.

From architecture to puritanism

New England cultivates its own – Old English – style, one which attracts tourists, the most enduring source of income, like magic

Architecture

Endless pine forests have always supplied New England with more wooden building material than it needed. Depending on the period in which they were built, the houses display either narrow diagonally nailed façade boards *(clapboard)* with small delicately sectioned windows – devoid of curtains – modest and low *(Cape Cod Style* and *Colonial Style)*, the roofs straight and steep *(Saltbox)*, trumpet their affluence with columns, balconies and roofed terraces *(Georgian)* or reveal a Neo-Gothic flair *(Victorian)*.

The predominant colour is white. But also typical is the dull blood-red or bluish grey. Fragile looking white picket fences all around have become the hallmark of the region.

Farmhouses and barns were raised mainly with noticeable hipped gable roofs. Many have been restored and transformed into cosy living quarters.

Wood is also the material used for a peculiarity in the history of construction: covered bridges.

The elite Harvard university

The basic idea behind this intricate construction is only logical. It protects not only travellers but also the bridge itself from rain and snow.

Fauna

New England's animal world is a part of that biosphere that stretches itself as one great forest belt across the entire North American continent. Within it live elk and black bears, beaver and skunk, white-tail deer and racoons. The cold waters of the Atlantic Ocean are abundant with much sought after crustaceans such as lobster as well as various dolphin types and varieties of whale. The main route of American migratory birds runs right over New England which is the reason why in spring and autumn more than 400 species can be tallied, among them Canadian geese flying in V-formation, their shrill cry filling the air.

Flora

New England's most famous plants are its deciduous trees whose leaves change colours magnificently in September and October from north to south ushering in au-

11

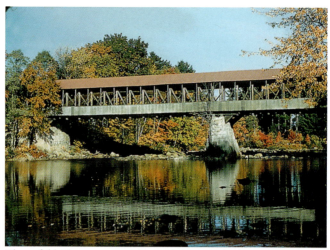
The roofed bridges are a rare sight outside New England

tumn – a colour spectacular made up of maple, birch, oak, beech and hickory. Pine and other evergreens complete the picture. Two thousand flowers, grasses and ferns are indigenous to the area. rhododendron, dogwood and cat's tails bloom as wild flowers. Blueberries (in Maine) and cranberries (in Massachusetts) have even developed into an economic factor of their own.

Native Americans

The original inhabitants of America crossed the Bering Straits from Asia some 12,000 years ago. As they had no written language and few developed technical crafts in today's sense of the term, they left little behind, with the possible exception of landscape designations. The number of Algonquin Indians, who first migrated to New England in the 15th century, amounted to some 25,000 when they first met the pilgrim fathers. They were fragmented into ten tribes. The most important: *Narragansetts* in Rhode Island, the *Pennacocks* in New Hampshire, the *Massachusetts* in

---

Autumn in flames – just give a call

In order that everyone can see the colourful panorama of his or her choice, tourist agencies in some states have instituted a call centre where from anywhere inside the continental US you can call and inquire as to the status of the leaves' colouring. The numbers are: 1/800/258 36 08 (New Hampshire), 1/800/282 68 63 (Connecticut), 1/800/227 62 77 (Massachusetts), 1/800/533 95 95 (Maine), 1/800/556 24 84 (Rhode Island). In Vermont (pay call): 802/828 32 39.

the state that still bears their name and the *Penobscot* in Maine. They lived not only from hunting but also from agriculture (beans, pumpkins, tobacco and maize). Early friendship with the settlers changed to enmity and death. Many of the original inhabitants were baptized and adapted, disappearing into the mixtures of peoples, the Americans. Today some 20,000 Indians live in New England, approximately one third of them, on reservations. Their political "special status" has allowed members of two tribes in Connecticut to open profitable gambling establishments.

Autumn
The one-of-a-kind colour display, the autumnal turning of the leaves is not scheduled exactly according to the calendar. Autumn rains and storms are quick to whisk the multicoloured leaves from the trees. As a rule the leaves begin to change in the northern New England states of Maine, Vermont and New Hampshire at the end of September, however, in Connecticut, Rhode Island and Massachusetts in October. The areas in which the natural display is most spectacular are the Berkshires in western Massachusetts and northwestern Connecticut and the mountainous landscape of New Hampshire (White Mountains) and Vermont (Green Mountains).

Ivy League
With around 250 colleges and universities, 13 per cent of all American students are enrolled here. Not only the elite universities of the *Ivy League*, as the sports and tradition-oriented colleges Harvard, Yale and Dartmouth are called, draw those eager for an education from all parts of the US: many a small town lives from its educational institutions, which, as is in America customary, are in private hands and require tuition. In the greater Boston metropolitan area alone, the income from this sector is estimated at some 2 billion dollars annually.

National Park
Only one of America's 54 "National Parks" is located in New England: *Acadia* in Maine. Yet it is, with over 3 three million visitors annually, one of the most popular. Rare animals live in the nature preserves of America and plants are, for the most part, unimpaired and free from human manipulation. A vast host of forest caretakers, called *rangers*, devotes itself to the care and cultivation of flora and fauna.

The more that the values of conservationists became rooted in common thinking, the more numerous were the areas designated *national forests, national seashores* or *national recreation areas*, and thus removed from private hands to be preserved for the good of all. Many states created *State Parks* with similar restriction without federal prompting.

Politics and the Law
The federal system of government in the US guarantees the 50 independent states a great deal of freedom, particularly in matters of education and penal codes. Some New England states are among the few across the country without capital punishment

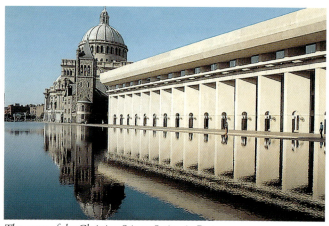

The centre of the Christian Science Society in Boston

(New Hampshire), others grant women the right of abortion (Connecticut). Many practice at the local level so-called "grass-roots democracy" through town meetings, in which, for instance, the municipal budget is determined. Distrust vis-à-vis all government is quite the normal thing in New England, with the result being that the sole independent congressman in 2-Party America comes from Vermont while in Maine an independent resides in the governor's mansion.

Puritanism

As the Puritans were oppressed in England, the promise of an uninhabited country was a powerful attraction. They sought a land where their own dogmatic values of penitence, moral living and the fear of God could become the foundation of the community. The material and spiritual life were together one; love of learning and divinely sanctioned striving for wealth were among their basic principles.

As much as freedom of belief may have been paramount for the Puritans themselves, the intolerance they displayed towards other persuasions and confessions, such as Quakers, Catholics or Jews was initially extreme. Going so far as torture, banishment or extermination. Even today the basic values of the Puritan way of life have maintained themselves, especially within the upper class of the old-resident families. They are known as *WASPs: white Anglo-Saxon Protestants.*

Other groups known for their strictness in religious matters have also left their mark: *Christian-Science-Society*, which spread throughout Boston, or the Quakers offshoot *Shakers*, who in their settlements elevated manual labour to a form of worship. The growing number of Catholic immigrants from Ireland, Italy and Portugal has failed to break the Protestant hegemony, even more than one half of

The church still has a say in many parts

New England's inhabitants are of the Roman Catholic faith and see the Pope as their spiritual head.

Economy

The lumber trade, agriculture, fishing and the manufacturing and processing industry are, in addition to tourism, the major money-makers in New England, which was hard hit by the last serious recession in 1991. The reason: industry lived for years from lucrative government defence contracts – today these are on the ebb. At the same time the major banks and insurance concerns located here incurred huge debts in risky real estate deals during the then ongoing boom. To top things off, the finance heads of many states were obliged to curtail expenditures due to decreasing tax revenues. The slack period is now past. But the one constant which prevents business cycle problems from becoming too serious in New England is one source of proceeds which never fails: tourism. The agricultural sector is also stable thanks to the cranberry (Massachusetts), potatoes and blueberries (Maine), milk and cheese (Vermont).

In the spirit of Marco Polo

Marco Polo was the first true world traveller. He travelled with peaceful intentions forging links between the East and the West. His aim was to discover the world, and explore different cultures and environments without changing or disrupting them. He is an excellent role model for the travellers of today and the future. Wherever we travel we should show respect for other peoples and the natural world.

WWF

SEAHORSE FISHO

967-1950
1989

LOBSTE

Lobster galore

New England's lobsters are famous. Lobster arrives on the table in every imaginable variation

New England's sense for the traditional has prevented fast-food branches from gaining a foothold outside of the larger cities. Instead, the region draws its nourishment from what is fished directly before the door, hunted, harvested or prepared fresh. Especially delightful are the culinary specialities offered in those spots close to the ocean: *lobster*, clams, baked fish, (e.g. *cod*) in all possible variations. The price asked for lobster is amazingly reasonable, especially along the seaboard. There you'll find *lobster pounds*, in which the tasty crustaceans are kept in tanks until they pass over through billowing steam to waiting plates. You select your choice by size and order *fries* as a side dish and perhaps cold beer and enjoy your feast out on wooden benches with a grandiose view of the oceans before you.

Among New England's specialities are also desserts, particularly fruit *pies.* Also characteristic of cuisine is: cheddar cheese from Vermont, prepared according to an Old English recipe or young goat cheese.

Several New England products are made into spices or refined into appetizers. Especially popular is the maple syrup, naturally sweet with additives. The syrup is extracted in springtime when the maple trees are tapped.

Breakfast at a coffee shop includes coffee, even if it's a bit thinner than the European norm. With coffee come eggs: scrambled, sunny side up, once over-easy or poached and bacon or ham home fries and toast.

In a proper restaurant, i.e. as opposed to the coffee shop, you are not allowed to seat yourself. You'll be assigned a table by the *maitre d'.*

Usually there is a lunch menu with sandwiches and soups; lunch prices lie considerably lower than those found on the *dinner menu.*

The waiter or waitress usually receives a tip. This is more than just a way of saying "thank you", it is a good part of that person's wages. The amount (minimum: 15 per cent) is printed in the menu along with the VAT (sales tax) which differs from state to state 5 per cent to 8.25 per cent.

Lobster – don't miss the popular crustacean cuisine during your travels

Folklore, collectibles and outlet shopping

Typically New England:
useful things and old stuff attract the souvenir hunter

The frugality of the New England Yankees is proverbial. Paired with a sense for tradition, you'll discover a speciality you'll stumble over on every street corner: *tag sales*, also called *yard sales*. This is nothing more than a privately organized mini flea market on which interesting collectibles and sometimes even valuable antiques turn up. The hunt for little antique trophies is one of the most popular pastimes of Americans on holiday. In the more remote areas of New England you'll meet so many drop-outs, escapees from the so-called "rat race", who make their living by selling arts and crafts, make pottery, weave carpets or create furniture. You'll find them in their workshops or at the many *Arts and Crafts Fairs.* The *Outlet Stores*, also offer a purchasing experience both typical and not to be missed. These stores are outlets of larger garment or footwear firms. The *Outlet Stores* with their bargains have done much to change the face of places like North Conway (New Hampshire), Manchester (Vermont) or Freeport and Kittery (Maine).

Your Shopping experience is not complete without a visit to a *General Store*, one of those old-time corner shops where one can satisfy (almost) every daily need.

Clothes sizes: for the ladies, US 6 = UK 8; US 8 = UK 10 etc. The sizes for gentlemen are identical in both countries; gentlemen's shoes: one size larger: British 10 = American 11; ladies' shoes 1 $\frac{1}{2}$ size larger: UK 5 = US 6 $\frac{1}{2}$.

On top of the price comes – with the exception of New Hampshire – VAT, so-called *(sales tax)*. In Connecticut it amounts to 6 per cent, in Maine 5.5 per cent, in Massachusetts 5 per cent, in New York (Long Island) 8.25 per cent, in Rhode Island 7 per cent and in Vermont 5 per cent.

Most shops are open from 10 am to 6 pm, including Saturdays. In *outlet stores* you may find them open on Sunday as well.

Little shops offer special things. New England has much to offer fishermen and hunters

19

Pride in history and tradition

New England celebrates Washington's Birthday just as majestically as a rowing contest at the elite schools

PUBLIC HOLIDAYS

On the following days government and state offices, post offices, schools and businesses are closed:

1 January *New Year's Day*

Last Monday in May *Memorial Day* (in honour of the war dead)

4 July *Independence Day* (National Holiday)

First Monday in September *Labor Day*

Fourth Thursday in November *Thanksgiving*

25 December *Christmas Day* (only one day is a holiday)

On the following days government and state offices are closed, offices are open and many businesses in the larger cities arranges special sales activities:

Third Monday in January *Martin Luther King's Birthday*

Third Monday in February *Presidents' Day*

In tradition-faithful New England, all festivals are celebrated in style – historical uniforms are a must here

Second Monday in October *Columbus Day* (in memory of Columbus' discovery of America)

First Tuesday in November *Election Day*

11 November *Veterans' Day*

EVENTS

January
Stowe (VT): Winter Carnival and Dog-Sled Racing

February
Old Sturbridge (MA): Washington's Birthday Celebration. Historica-pageant about the first president

March
All over Vermont: Maple Sugar Events. Tours of maple syrup factories

April
Boston (MA): Boston Marathon
Concord (NH): Parade on Patriot's Day, anniversary of the first battle in the War for Independence against the British

May
Boston: Hidden Gardens of Beacon Hill. Guided tour through the most beautiful city gardens

21

Salem (MA): Salem Seaport Festival. Entertainment, art and a culinary tasting tour through local restaurants

Brimfield (CT): More than 400 dealers meet (also at the beginning of July as well as the middle of Sept.) for an open-air antiques sale.

June

Farmington (CT): Farmington Antiques Weekend. Huge antique and collectibles market

New London (CT): Yale-Harvard Regatta, Rowing contest of the two elite universities

Portsmouth (NH): Open-air jazz festival Ceres Street in the harbour

Bar Harbor (ME): Bar Harbor Days. Summer amusement where a lobster chase is staged and the fishing boats are christened

★ *Boston: Harbor festival.* In the week preceding Independence Day (4 July), more than 200 events take place at the harbour.

July

Fourth of July: On *Independence Day* there are parades everywhere, picnics and festivities, often with fireworks and music

Hancock (MA): Shaker Crafts Festival. Demonstration of old handicraft techniques

Lenox (MA): Tanglewood Music Festival. Open-air classical concert sponsored by the Boston Symphony Orchestra

Rockland (ME): Schooner Days. Three days long, everything revolves around water and sports

Newport (RI): Newport Tennis Week. The *Miller Lite Tournament* takes place on the green of the Tennis Hall of Fame

★ *Boothbay Harbor (ME): Windjammer Days.* Parade of large and small sailboats

★ *Newport (RI): Music Festival.* Two weeks of concerts

August

Newbury (NH): League of New Hampshire Craftsmen's Fair. Creators of arts and handicrafts from the Mount Sunapee State Park area present their work

★ *Rockland (ME): Maine Lobster Festival.* Three days of nothing but lobsters

Newport (RI): Jazz Festival in the Fort Adams State Park

Gloucester (MA): Waterfront Festival. Art and handicrafts at the historic Atlantic harbour

Hancock Shaker Village (MA): Antiques Show. Antiques are on view in the gigantic round barn of the shaker

A long cold one on draft

The *Great New England Brewers Festival* in Northampton (MA) in June, the *Vermont Brewers Festival in Burlington (VT)* in July or the *Grand Old Portsmouth Fall Brewer's Festival (NH)* at the end of September all have one thing in common: they celebrate the products of the smaller breweries, called "micro breweries" in the US, which product their delicious nectar according to German or English recipes. Whoever misses a can also find beers such as ale stout or lager at the supermarket or at better restaurants. The top brands are considered Hammer & Nail (CT), Otter Cree (CT) and The Shipyard (ME).

MARCO POLO SELECTION: FESTIVALS

1 **Boothbay Harbor: Windjammer Days**
Parade of the Big Ships (page 22)

2 **Boston: Harbor Festival**
Over 200 events in the harbour and surrounding area (page 22)

3 **New Haven: Fall Antiques Show**
One of the largest antique fairs in the country. Meeting place for collectors (page 23)

4 **Newport Music Festival**
Concerts at historical sites (page 22)

5 **Rockland: Maine Lobster Festival**
Fun: can't get enough simply three days of downing lobsters (page 22)

Sugarbush (VT): Folk Festival

Bridgehampton (Long Island): Hampton Classic Horse Show. Riding contest and charity function with many VIPs

East Hampton (Long Island): Artists and Writers. Famous artists and writers play in softball tournament

September

Newport (RI): Annual Classic Regatta. Over 100 Boats built between the end of the 19th century and 1995 sail in Narrangansett Bay for the championship

Goshen (CT): At the *Goshen Fair* farmers display their prize-winning produce and compete in old-fashioned events such as chopping wood

Cambridge (MA): Cambridge River Festival. Folk and jazz, jugglers and magicians on the banks of the Charles River

★ *New Haven (CT): Fall Antiques Show,* an absolute "must" for antique collectors in New England

Harwich (MA): Harwich Cranberry Festival. Festivals at cranberry harvest time with parade and fireworks

Brattleboro (VT): Brattleboro Arts Festival. Shortly before the highpoint of the leaves' changing, among other activities boat trips on the Connecticut River

October

South Carver (MA): Harvest Festival on the occasion of the cranberry harvest with tours through the fields

East Hampton (Long Island): Hampton's International Film Festival. High-class movie-fan get-together

Northeast Kingdom (VT): Foliage Festivals when the leaves change in northeastern Vermont

November

Plymouth (MA): A public *Thanksgiving Day Dinner* in memory of the first Thanksgiving of the Pilgrims

December

Boston (MA): Re-enactment of the 1773 Boston Tea Party

Boston (MA): The *First Night* (New Year's Eve without alcoholic beverages) transforms the city into one gigantic street party

Water, wind and untamed forests

In Connecticut and Rhode Island travellers find a striking contrast: a sense of timelessness along with well-to-do residents

The state with the highest per capita income in the US, the biggest concentration of millionaires and a reputation for money-making industriousness and ingenuity has the typical

On the Connecticut River

dual aspects of a "borderstate": Connecticut. For thousands of commuters working in nearby New York, it offers the stylish serenity of green New England. For concerned Yankee traditionalists, Connecticut is in danger of losing its character amid a maze of busy streets and shop-

Hotel and restaurant prices

Hotels
Category 1: Inns and hotels over $150
Category 2: Inns and hotels from $100 to $150
Category 3: Inns and better motels under $100

The prices are valid for two persons in a double. Rooms in simple motels cost generally $75. The toll-free reservation number of some motel chains:
Best Western 1/800/528 12 34
Choice Hotels (Comfort and Quality Inn) 1/800/221 22 22
Days Inn 1/800/325 25 25

Hampton Inn 1/800/426 78 66
Ramada Inn 1/800/272 62 32
The recommendations are valid foremost for classical New England inns: stylish, but also with thin walls, often stuffed with antiques. Their (listed) prices are between the beginning of June and the end of Sept., otherwise noticeably reduced.

Restaurants
Category 1: over $50
Category 2: from $25 to $50
Category 3: under $25
The prices include a dinner with starters, main course and dessert.

MARCO POLO SELECTION: CONNECTICUT AND RHODE ISLAND

1 Block Island and its beaches
Best in June or September (page 27)

2 Bowen's Wharf in Newport
Rhode Islands most beautiful businesses and restaurants (page 36)

3 Foxwoods Casino
Indians run the most successful casino in the world (page 36)

4 Gilded Age Newport
Newport's Golden Mile. The Summer palaces of railway tycoons (page 35)

5 Litchfield and Surroundings
New England classic, quite special during autumn (page 31)

6 Mystic Seaport
Maritime masterpieces and noble junk shopping (page 33)

ping centres. Those same streets, however, provide the state's inhabitants with easy and comfortable access to the cultivated old towns and villages that convey, to every visitor coming from New York, the first unforgettable impression of New England's timelessness. This atmosphere is found in the hills of Litchfield in the northwest and the Connecticut River Valley, in the fishing villages on Long Island Sound and the moor land in the eastern part of the state.

New England's largest river, the *Connecticut River*, which has its source in the northeastern corner of New Hampshire, was called *Quinnehtukqut* by the Mohicans, the "place with the river that obeys the tides". It attracted British settlers right from the beginning. Stern Puritans, for whom the life in Boston was too free and easy, founded the towns of Hartford, Windsor and Wethersfield one after another

on the banks of the Connecticut. As an independent colony, they soon drew up a constitution, the memory of which is still today evident to all: Connecticut's state motto as emblazoned on every license plate reads, *Constitution State*.

From clocks and locks to bikes and pistols on to jet propulsion systems and atomic submarines, Connecticut has delivered just about everything that spurs America on and keeps her in motion. A resounding certificate of achievement for the third smallest federal state in the Union. An adequate comparison to the 12,000 sq km state is difficult to find anywhere on the globe.

The tiniest independent political entity in the US is right next door: Rhode Island. The origin of the name remains in dispute. Some refer to the travels of the Dutch seafarer Adrian Block and his description of a "red island". Others prefer to think of the Greek island of Rhodes as godfather.

Undisputed, however, remains the fact that Rhode Island was founded as an isle of tolerance – safe haven for the Quakers and Baptists from the religious dictates of the Puritans. The great majority placed their fortunes on overseas trade (concentration: rum and slaves). It was later, with a population of one million, that it became the most densely populated state in the US (320 inhabitants per sq km) and a centre of the growing textile industry. Today places like Charlestown (East Beach), Matunuck, Narragansett, Little Compton (Goosewing Beach) and above all Newport thanks to their clean beaches, attractive sailing domains and abundant fishing grounds. Water has remained in the *Ocean State* life's elixir non plus ultra.

BLOCK ISLAND

(109/D5) ★ The truly pleasant thing about this island, named after its Dutch discoverer and abounding in rolling meadows and old stone walls, is its ability to keep tourism under firm control. The 10-km-long island can only be reached by ferry from New London in Connecticut, Montauk Point on Long Island, likewise from Newport, Providence and Judith Point in Rhode Island. In Old Harbor you find hotels from the Victorian Period, businesses and restaurants. New Harbor offers anchorage for yachts and fishing boats. The most beautiful beach: Crescent Beach.

At sunrise the view from ◁◁ Mohegan Bluffs on the southern tip of the island, also called "The Block" is especially stunning. The best place for *people watching* is the terrace of the Harborside Inn.

SIGHTS

Block Island Historical Society
An overview of the island's history. *Old Town Rd.; June–Sept. daily 10 am–4 pm; Tel. 401/ 466 24 81*

HOTELS

Atlantic Inn
Victorian House with restaurant. A good number of the 21 rooms have a ◁◁ view over the harbour. *High St., Block Island; Tel. 401/466 58 83; Fax 466 56 78; category 1–2*

The Hotel Manisses/The 1661 Inn
The hotel, circa 1870, is, architecturally speaking, the Grand Old Lady of the island. Rooms with a view over the harbour. *Outstanding restaurant: the Manisses.* *Hotel: 17 rooms; Inn: 21 rooms; Spring St., Block Island; Tel. 401/466 20 63; Fax 466 31 62; category 1–2*

SPORTS & LEISURE

Bicycles
Old Harbor Bike Shop, at the ferry pier; Tel. 401/466 20 29

Hiking
The island is criss-crossed with hiking trails and bike paths. Particularly nice is the ◁◁ *Clayhead Nature Trail all along the cliffs on the east side of the island*

**Block Island
Chamber of Commerce**

1 Water St.; Mon–Fri 9 am–4 pm, during the summer also Fri, Sat 9 am–5 pm and Sun 11 am–2 pm; Tel. 401/466 29 82

CORNWALL

(**108/B4**) The *Housatonic River*, the second largest river in Connecticut, likewise *Mohawk Mountain* set their stamp on the landscape of the southern approaches to the richly wooded *Berkshires.* With its rapids, the river lures wild-water enthusiasts as well as fishermen eager for a trout trophy. Trekking paths draw over the hills, below the famous Appalachian Trail, leading from Arkansas to Maine. Among Cornwall's attractions is a roofed bridge from the year 1864 in West Cornwall and the ski slopes up on Mohawk Mountain (500 m above sea level).

Mainstreet in little West Cornwall (Route 128) beams out all the charm of pleasant New England activity. Here, a rustic *coffee shop* (The Station House Cafe), a shop with *Ceramics* (Cornwall Bridge Pottery), another shop for *antique books* (Barbara Farnsworth Bookseller), artistic *furniture in Shaker-Style* from the workshop of Ian Ingersoll (in the one-time Bridge customs house, *Tel. 860/672 63 34),* a shop with *all the needs of the sports-and-fly fishing enthusiast,* licenses for trout fishing likewise provided, and the *Antiques of Michael Trapp* (River Rd.).

Hilltop Haven B & B

Spectacular view of the Berkshire Mountains. *2 rooms;*

Timeless congeniality in small fishing ports, high-rises in Hartford

175 Dibble Hill Rd., West Cornwall; Tel. and Fax 860/672 68 71; category 1–2

SPORTS & LEISURE

Kanus
Clarke Outdoors, West Cornwall (Route 7; Tel. 860/672 63 65), rents boats for the rapids excursion on the Housatonic and organizes the transportation.

ESSEX AND THE VALLEY OF THE CONNECTICUT RIVER

(108/C5–4) From the old seaport Essex you view the *Lower Connecticut Valley,* formed by Ice Age glaciers. The towns originated in the early 18th century when trade on the rivers experienced its heyday. As second money-maker alongside farming, ship building developed: more than 50 wharves were once sprinkled along the river, along which warships were built during the Civil War to assist in defeating the South. Deep River also boasts numerous antique dealers.

SIGHTS

Valley Railroad
After the train trip through the Connecticut River Valley, there's an excursion with the steamboat starting from Deep River. *Exit 3 from Route 9 or Exit 69 from the I-95, Essex; May–Oct. 12 am, 1.30 am and 3 pm; admission $10 with the steamer $16); Tel. 860/767 01 03*

HOTEL

Riverwind
Old farmhouse. *8 rooms; 209 Main St., Deep River; Tel. 860/526 20 14; Fax 526 08 75; category 1–3*

INFORMATION

Connecticut River Valley & Shoreline Visitors Council
393 Main St., Middletown; Mon–Fri 9 am–4.30 pm; Tel. 860/347 00 28

SURROUNDING AREA

Gilette Castle State Park   (108/C4)
North of Deep River lies the *Gilette Castle State Park* in Hadlyme *(67 River Rd.; Tel. 860/ 526 23 36)* with the 24-room granite castles (1919) of the actor William Gilette, modelled after the fortresses of German knights.

Goodspeed Opera House   (108/C4)
A few kilometres up river stands the *Goodspeed Opera House* (1876), in which theatre performances are still put on today. The imposing structure with the river in the foreground is a popular photo background. *Route 82, East Haddam*

HARTFORD

(108/C4) The 138,000 strong capital of Connecticut is known in America as the centre of the insurance industry. What was once home to authors Mark Twain and Harriet Beecher Stowe in the 19th century, today evinces typical American big-city problems: affluence and urban decline lie dangerously close to

Sky-scrapers in Hartford

America: *Uncle Tom's Cabin*. Both buildings illustrate, with furniture and mementoes, the style of living and the mood of the 19th century. *351 Farmington Ave. (Exit 46 off the I-84); Mon, Wed to Sat 9.30 am–5 pm, Sun 12 am –5 pm; admission for Twain $9; Tel. 860/493 64 11; for Beecher Stowe $6.50; Tel. 860/525 93 17*

Wadsworth Atheneum

The oldest public art museum in the US with works by Winslow Homer to Andy Warhol. Excellent restaurant in the museum building. *600 Main St.; Tues–Sun 11 am–5 pm; admission $7; Tel. 860/278 26 70*

SURROUNDING AREA

Old Wethersfield   (108/C4)

In Old Wethersfield, southeast of Hartford on Route 99, three well kept old homes form a museum:

One of the houses, the *Joseph Webb House* (1752), was used by George Washington, first American president, as a conference location. *Webb-Dean-Stevens-Museum, 211 Main St.; Tel. 860/529 06 12; admission $8.* Also worth seeing is the *Buttolph-Williams House (249 Broad St.; Tel. 860/529 04 60)* built in the year 1692, its kitchen is the best preserved of the era.

LAKEVILLE AND SALISBURY

(108/B4) In farmland amid the soft hills of northwestern Connecticut lies the well-to-do dual township that with its white manor houses and thorough-

each other. Skyscrapers visibly etch out the skyline in the Connecticut River Valley. But whoever makes the effort to look more closely recognizes too that the restructuring from industrial base (say, the weapons manufacturer Colt) to service centre has come short of its goal. One attractive legacy of the city fathers are the parks. Hartford's proportion of park area is larger than in any other large American city.

SIGHTS

Mark Twain House (Nook Farm)

In the Victorian Villa the popular writer *Mark Twain* brought *Tom Sawyer* and *Huckleberry Finn* to life. Next-door lived *Harriet Beecher Stowe*, author of the much-read classic describing the state of human beings under slavery in fares with well-tended gardens offers a typical picture of picturesque New England. Today, few have an inkling that the prosperity was derived from iron extraction and smelting. And that affluence has apparently become a fact in spite of itself. Nowadays rich double-home owners from New York, authors as well as private schools set the tone for the solid, respectable "good life".

For a stopover on route 41 the coffee shop *Mount Riga* welcomes guests in Lakeville as does the tea room *Chaiwalla* in Salisbury.

RESTAURANTS

The Boat House

Oysters and hamburgers, but typical New England dishes as well. *349 Main St. (Routes 41 and 44), Lakeville; Tel. 860/435 21 11; category 2*

Charlotte

In an old house surrounded by antiques you are served new creations. The antiques are also for sale. *223 Main St., Lakeville; Tel. 860/435 35 51; category 2*

HOTEL

Under Mountain Inn

The white farmhouse is bursting with antiques. Breakfast and lunch are included. *7 rooms; 482 Under Mountain Rd. (Route 41), Salisbury; Tel. 860/435 02 42; Fax 435 23 79; category 1*

LITCHFIELD

(108/B4) ★ Litchfield is the perfect example of a living New England small town. Following its heyday in the 19th century, interest on the preservation and maintenance of the stately white residences arose. Many of the houses along the North and

Hartford's capitol: Connecticut's gubernatorial residence and seat of parliament

South Main Street were built in the 18th century. In *Tapping Reeve House (82 South St.)* Litchfield Law School was based, visited later by many high-ranking politicians. The lawn was laid out more than 100 years ago by landscapers. History comes alive in the *Litchfield Historical Society Museum; (South St./East St.; Tues–Sat 11 am–5 pm, Sun 1 pm–5 pm; Tel. 860/567 45 01)*. For an especially charming experience, visit the 7000-soul settlement *Congregational Church* (1829), most atmospheric when the leaves begin to change.

RESTAURANT

West Street Grill
A bistro with regional kitchen set between attractive shops and better galleries. *43 West St.; Tel. 860/567-38 85; category 2*

HOTEL

Tollgate Hill Inn and Restaurant
Tavern from the year 1745 located on the old stagecoach route to Albany; today a cosy inn with restaurant. *20 rooms; Tollgate Rd./Route 202, Litchfield; Tel. 860/567-45 45; Fax 567-83 97; category 1–2 (hotel) and 2 (restaurant)*

SPORTS & LEISURE

Swimming
❂ In the lake at *Mount Tom State Park (Route 202 southwesterly)*

INFORMATION

Litchfield Hills Travel Council
Information stand at *Village Green; June–Oct. daily 5 am–5 pm*

SURROUNDING AREA

Lake Waramaug (108/B4)
Connecticut's second largest natural lake is called in the Indian language "a good place for fishing". A number of inns have established themselves around the lake. They offer a beautiful view 🌊 over the water surrounded by thick woods and a kitchen well worth trying. Among the best are: *Boulder's Inn (East Shore Rd., New Preston; Tel. 860/868 05 41; category 1); Hopkins Inn (22 Hopkins Rd., New Preston; Tel. 860/868 72 95; category 2)* with recipes from Switzerland and the *Lakeview Inn (107 North Shore Rd.; Tel. 860/868 10 00; category 1)* with outstanding lobster and lamb dishes. Nearby you'll find the *Hopkins Vinery*, with respectable white wines.

The attraction of New Preston: antique stores. Many are to be found along Route 45 between Lake Waramaug and Route 202.

MYSTIC

(109/D4–5) Founded as a fishing village in 1649, Mystic became a centre of ship building following the first half of the 19th century. *Route 27 leads to Old Mystic with its original buildings and a main street full of shops with hand-made wares and gifts.*

SIGHTS

Mystic Marinelife Aquarium
Underwater zoo with some 6000 different animals, among them whales, dolphins and seals. *55 Coogan Blvd. (Exit 90 of the I-95); daily 9 am–5 pm; admissions $13; Tel. 860/572 59 55*

Mystic Seaport Museum

★ This sea travel and fishing museum houses a replica of a 19th century coastal village – a significant aspect of New England history. Among the ships lying at anchor is the one and only existent wooden whaling boat, the "Charles W. Morgan" (1841). *75 Greenmanville Ave. (Exit 90 off the I-95); May–Oct. daily 9 am–5 pm; Nov–April 9 am–4 pm; admission $16; Tel. 860/572 07 11*

RESTAURANTS

Abbott's Lobster in the Rough

Lobster feasting at simple wooden tables under the open sky. You bring along your own wine and beer. *117 Pearl St., Noank; Tel. 860/536-7719; category 3*

Flood Tide Restaurant

On a small rise in *The Inn at Mystic*, with a view of the harbour. Fish, noodle dishes, steaks. *Route 1/Route 27; Tel. 860/536 81 40; category 2*

HOTELS

The Inn at Mystic

The old house with motel annex offers two price classes. *68 rooms; Route 1/Route 27, Mystic; Tel. 860/536 96 04; Fax 572 16 35; category 1–2*

The Old Mystic Inn

Quiet house from the year 1826 only a few kilometres from the tourist fuss. *8 rooms; 52 Main St., Old Mystic; Tel. 860/572 94 22; Fax 572 99 54; category 1–2*

INFORMATION

Mystic Tourist Information

Olde Mystic Village Mall, *Coogan Blvd. (Exit 90 off the I-95); daily 10 am–5 pm, in the summer 9 am–6 pm; Tel. 860/536 16 41*

Mystic was earlier the centre of ship building in the northern US

NARRAGANSETT

(109/D 4) The small town of the southwestern coast of Rhode Island was a rich spa at the end of the 19th century as well as stopover for steamers between New York and Newport. Today it's the beaches that draw the crowds. Worth seeing: *Lighthouse of Point Judith* and the trip there along the coast.

HOTELS

Stonelea
More than 100 years old. Beautiful antiques. ❧ View to the sea. *7 rooms; no credit cards; 40 Newton Ave., Narragansett; Tel. 401/ 783 95 46; Fax 792 82 37; category 1*

SPORTS & LEISURE

Beaches
From routes 1 and 1 A you reach the following beaches: *South County Atlantic Beach Park (near Watch Hill), East Beach in Charlestown Beachway State Park, East Beach and Moonstone Beach (near Charlestown), Roy Carpenter's Beach, Matunuck Beach and Matunuck State Beach (near Matunuck) as well as near Point Judith the Roger W. Wheeler Memorial Beach.*

INFORMATION

South County Tourism Council
4808 Tower Hill Rd., Wakefield; Mon–Fri 9 am–5 pm; Tel. 401/ 789 44 22

NEW HAVEN

(108/C5) Famous as the location of Yale University, which, besides Harvard, is considered the best educational institution in the US.

SIGHTS

Sights for the visitor: a series of museums which constantly acquire new items due to the generosity of former students. The *Yale University Art Gallery* houses art works from Old Egypt to the present day *(Tel. 203/432 06 00)*. The *Yale Center for British Art (Tel. 203/432 28 00)* boasts the largest collection of British art outside of the UK. The *Beinecke Rare Book Library (Tel. 203/432 29 77)* is the largest library in the world for rare books and manuscripts. *Guided tours over the university campus* are organized *(New Haven Green, 149 Elm St.; Tel. 203/432 23 00)*. Sought-after Yale souvenirs are found in the *Yale Coop (924 Chapel St.; Tel. 203/772 22 00)*.

NEWPORT

(109/D–E4) Founded in the year 1639 by religious splinter groups, Newport developed into an important harbour and trading city. The nobility of the finance world and railway barons from New York set the finishing touches on the already splendid face of the city by adding one noteworthy feature: large stone residences which served as summer villas and were called with false modesty *cottages*. The pomp of that bygone era, concentrated on Ocean Drive and Bellevue Avenue, finds proper contrast in the reserved but distinctive affluence of the wooden *colonial houses* on Washington Square

International sailing point: the Newport harbour

and Broadway. The artfully decorated entranceways are particularly delightful. Among the sights are the *Hunter House* from 1748 *(54 Washington St.; May–Sept. daily 10 am–5 pm; admission $9; Tel. 401/847 10 00).*

Newport can be explored either on foot or by bike. The ✹ *Cliff Walk* leads from the eastside of Newport along the sea passing by the rear gardens of the mansions. *Ocean Drive* also offers brief glimpses of the "better life". One good destination: the terrace of the *Inn at Castle Hill.* ✹ Gazing out upon Narragansett Bay with a glass of gin tonic in hand, one can dream of Newport's golden times.

SIGHTS

The Astor's Beechwood
Former summer palace of the Astor clan, in which actors, clad in historical costumes, act out would-be scenes from the "family life" of the wealthy. *580 Bellevue Ave.; daily 10 am–5 pm; admission $8.75; Tel. 401/846-37 72*

Gilded Age Newport
★ Six summer palaces of turn of the iron-and-steel magnates today belong to the *Preservation Society of Newport* and can be visited. The most impressive: *The Breakers,* the house of Cornelius Vanderbilt II. with 70 rooms *(Ochre Point Ave.).* 2,500 workmen required two years to complete the gilded opulence. *April–Oct. daily 10 am–5 pm; admission $12; addresses and tickets ($47 for all ten houses): Newport Preservation Society; Tel. 401/847 10 00*

Hammersmith Farm
The 28-room summer house of the family *Auchincloss.* Jacqueline Kennedy Onassis, born Auchincloss, grew up here. In her little girl's room personal objects and drawings can be viewed. During the presidency of John F. Kennedy, Hammersmith Farm was the presidential summer residence. *Ocean Drive near Fort Adams; April–Nov. daily 10 am–5 pm; admission $8; Tel. 401/846 73 46*

Tennis Hall of Fame

A tennis museum with mementoes from the history of the sport "in white". On the green a game costs $25. *194 Bellevue Ave.; 10 am–5 pm; admission $8; Tel. 401/849 39 90*

RESTAURANTS

Black Pearl

Cosy old tavern with terrace on the pier. Fish and duck from grill. *Bannister's Wharf; Tel. 401/846-52 64; category 2*

Clarke Cooke House

French-inspired Mediterranean cuisine in a house from the year 1790. ◁▷ View to the harbour. *Bannister's Wharf; Tel. 401/849-29 00, category 1*

Scales & Shells

Fish and lobster fresh from the grill. Reserve! *527 Thames St.; Tel. 401/846-34 74; category 3*

SHOPPING

★ Along *Bowen's* and *Bannister's Wharf* are strung boutiques, galleries and restaurants one after the other, while on the boat moorings the yachts of rich holiday-makers lie at anchor. Antique dealers are found on Thames and Spring Streets.

HOTELS

The Admirals

Three *inns* in historical buildings inside the old town centre. *43 rooms; Post address: 8 Fair St., Newport; Tel. 401/846 42 56; Fax 848 80 06; category 1–3*

The Francis Malbone House

Laura-Ashley style direct on the shore street. *18 rooms; 392 Thames St., Newport; Tel. 401/846 03 92; Fax 848 59 56; category 1*

The Ivy Lodge

Right next to the large summer palaces. Victorian charm. *8 rooms; 12 Clay St., Newport; Tel. 401/849 68 65; Fax 849 29 19; category 1–2*

Newport Gateway Hotel

Minimal motel comfort from $65. *47 rooms; 31 W Main Rd., Jamestown; Tel. 401/847 27 35; Fax 847 54 34; category 3*

Yankee Peddler Inn

B & B from the year 1830. *19 rooms; 113 Touro St., Newport; Tel. 401/846 13 23; Fax 849 04 26; category 1–3*

**Newport Country
Convention and Visitors Bureau**
*23 America's Cup Ave.; daily 9 am–
5 pm; Tel. 401/849 80 98*

OLD LYME

(108/C5) Former artist colony. In the
Florence Griswold Museum, named
for the patroness, who was also epi-
centre of the then art scene, diverse
paintings can be viewed *(96 Lyme
St.; Tel. 860/434 55 42)*.

RESTAURANTS

Two of Connecticut's most famous inns lie close to each other:
the *Bee and Thistle Inn (100 Lyme
St.; Tel. 860/434 16 67)* and the
*Old Lyme Inn (85 Lyme St.; Tel.
860/434 26 00)*. Both boast exquisite kitchens *(category 1–2)*.

SPORTS & LEISURE

Beaches
Connecticut's popular bathing
spots are in the *Hammonasset
Beach State Park (near Madison; Tel.
203/245-18 17)* and in *Rocky
Neck State Park Beach (near Niantic;
Tel. 860/739 54 71)*.

PROVIDENCE

(109/D4) The capital of Rhode Island (pop. 160,000) has a good
number of outstanding architectural facets, for example the *John
Brown House*, the one-time home of
a rich tradesman, built in 1786
*(52 Power St./Benefit St.; Tel.
401/331 85 75)* and the houses on
College Hill, which nicely demon-
strate the change in style from the
18th to 19th century. In the mu-

seum of the *Rhode Island School of
Design (RISD)* rewarding itinerant
exhibitions may be viewed dealing
mainly with textiles *(224 Benefit St.;
Tel. 401/454 65 00)*.

HOTEL

The Old Court Bed & Breakfast
Former clergyman's house with
ten rooms and ten fireplaces.
*144 Benefit St., Providence; Tel.
401/751 20 02; Fax 272 48 30;
category 2*

STONINGTON

(109/D5) Ex-shaling centre on a
peninsula in southeastern Connecticut. Stonington is, with its
Water Street, a well kept-up example of a coastal town in New England – including its Sleepy-Hol-
low atmosphere. Worth seeing:
the *Old Lighthouse Museum* with
whaling memorabilia.

RESTAURANT

Noah's
Here traditional and long out-of-
use ingredients are back in use
(e. g. ferns). *113 Water St., Stonington; Tel. 860/535 39 25; category 2*

HOTELS

Randall's Ordinary
House from the 17th century &
restaurant with home cooking
and lots of it. *15 rooms; Route 2;
North Stonington; Tel. 860/599
45 40; Fax 599 33 08; category 1–2*

Shelter Harbor Inn
Inn near the beach with a good
restaurant. *24 rooms; Route 1; 10
Wagner Rd., Westerl; Tel. 401/322
88 83; Fax 322 79 07; category 1–2*

Pace setter in the northeast

In the centre of New England: beaches, winter sports and old fishing ports

Massachusetts, named after the Indian tribe with which the settlers came into first contact, was always New England's forerunner. That began with the landing of the "Mayflower" in Plymouth (1620) and continued: the first university was established in *Harvard* (1636). Bostons *Common* became the first public park (1634), and here – in the largest city in New England, which today has 750,000 – the first underground in America rumbled off in 1898. Massachusetts is moreover the cradle of the American Revolution, which began with the Bostonians' protest against the taxing policy of the British colonial rulers and occurrences like the *Boston Massacre* (1770) and the *Boston Tea Party* (1773).

Because the state stretches from the mountainous Berkshires to the Atlantic islands *Martha's Vineyard* and *Nantucket* across the entire expanse of New England, it also offers a charming

Boston is the naval of the world. At least the old-time Bostonians are convinced of it

cross-section of the region – geographically and historically: from summer beaches to winter sport and from landmark industrial centres to old-established fishing villages, from meadows and fields to the woods ablaze with autumnal colours. Massachusetts symbolizes the development of the American northeast from agriculture and whaling to sea trade and industrialisation to computer design. Colleges and universities – alone in greater Boston there are more than 50 – provide steady and reliable sources of new intellectual potential.

As opposed to the other five New England states, Massachusetts, with 6 million inhabitants is large enough to make its voice heard at the federal level among the other, much larger members of the Union. Its most renowned politicians hail from one family. A family bearing the Irish name Kennedy and represents the mature Catholic influence in the region, which has been able to soften the stern Puritan origins. The name signifies still another tradition. The Kennedy Clan owns, like many Bostonians, a residence on *Cape Cod*. The peninsula was and has remained the most famous and most elegant holiday colony in the US.

BOSTON

☞ City Map inside back cover

(**109/E3**) The place that Boston has allotted itself in the global game is typically American. One views oneself simply as the *hub of the universe*, as the navel of the world. There's tradition to that. Boston was founded in 1630, when 1,000 Puritans, with their future governor John Winthrop at the head, landed at the point of the Massachusetts coast. After early attempts to claim Salem and Charlestown failed, they discovered the peninsula, then known as Shawmut, for themselves; previously an Anglican clergyman had been living a hermit's life on the spot. The town, first known for its hilly terrain, was later christened Boston, procticing the belief that state and church are one. Even if the Puritans themselves had been subjected to religious persecution in England, once in America they showed little inclination toward tolerance themselves. They punished everyone who offended against, for instance, the strict rules governing the Sabbath or those of the community at large by placing the unlucky sinner in the stocks. Incidentally, the first person placed in the stock was their constructor. He had demanded too high a price for his work.

Elitarian is a word which was never out of place in New England's largest city and only true metropolis. Here, where one once turned a cold shoulder to the

---

MARCO POLO SELECTION: MASSACHUSETTS

1 The Berkshires
The mountains around Lenox bear the nickname "Inland Newport" (page 51)

2 Boston: Freedom Trail
Through Boston on foot In the footprints of hsitory (page 42)

3 Cambridge: University Fair
Cafés and bookshops at and around Harvard Square (page 46)

4 Cape Cod: Beach time
Best of all: Wellfleet and Cape Cod National Seashore. Bostoner meetingpoint (page 46)

5 Hancock Shaker Village
Furniture design and handcrafts, fascinating in its simplicity and spiritualilty (page 57)

6 Romantic coast on Route 127 A
Fascination between Gloucester and Rockport (page 50)

7 Martha's Vineyard
Island with cliffs and beach Of the finest (page 52)

8 Nantucket
On the tracks of whalers and isolation. Time seems to stand still (page 54)

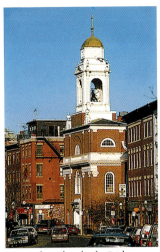

St Joseph's Church: the Irish immigrants left their mark

The colony's capital drew its prosperity from trade with England and the West Indies. Later, as one of the economy centres of the US, Boston blossomed thanks to trade with China and East Asia. Following a phase of decline at the beginning of the 20th century, the harbour was modernized and extended. Today, however, the city draws its affluence for the most part from the computer industry, banking and insurance enterprises and other service industries.

The harbour area has meanwhile become a veritable magnet for businesses, restaurants and museums eager to move into the renovated granite warehouses.

Departing a bit from this area, called the waterfront, North End presents itself. Traditionally the neighbourhood of Italian immigrants and Beacon Hill with its noble residences from the early 19th century.

Boston, like New York and San Francisco, is a city that one can explore easily on foot. The major attractions of the downtown lie close to each other, though the traffic grid is admittedly for new-comers a snarled maze of one-way streets. A practical aid in making the rounds is the *Freedom Trail,* a red line that runs right through the city and which leads, beginning at Boston Common, the expansive park, through state government and finance districts to the history-saturated spots of North End.

The underground net simplifies any and all ambitious excursions, linking the centre and the shopping streets in Back Bay

British Empire, America's intellectual elite was formed and at the same time carried on a profitable trade. Bostonians were always more open to the world and to culture, more historically aware and yet receptive to decisive developments of the times. It is also no coincidence that Boston is nearly the only city in the US with a museum devoted exclusively to computers.

In contrast to the immaculate white of the typical New England architecture, here a mighty urban landscape of red-brick buildings has reared up over the centuries. Along land which was won back from the sea, towered over by skyscrapers testifying to the latest building boom stands *downtown.* The houses of the hunchbacked Beacon Hill and North End, strewn, in places, with narrow and bumpy cobblestones, are the proud heritage of a time when America was still a part of Europe.

with the airport as well as Cambridge and Harvard.

Despite their reputation for reserve and snootiness, Bostonians are also a blend of worldliness and being well read, of Irish pub chumminess and Italian espresso charm, snobbish Brahman airs and nouveau-riche yuppiedom, who take a certain pleasure in meeting people. And it's worth making the effort to know them as well.

SIGHTS

Boston Harbour Cruises (U/F3)
The approximately three-quarter-hour harbour cruise with goods views of the skyline. *Every hour 10.30 am–4.30 pm; $8. In addition there are so-called Whale Watches: 5 hours; $28; 1 Long Wharf; Tel. 617/723 78 00*

Freedom Trail (U/D–E 4–1)
★ A red line on the pavement leads to 16 historical highlights. Among other things it leads to the *Old South Meeting House*, where the conspiring meeting leading up to the "Boston Tea Party" took place, to the *Old State House*, the seat of the Colonial Government and scene of the "Boston Massacre", to *Paul Revere House*, the residence of the illustrious freedom fighter and to the *"USS Constitution 12"*, the oldest warship of the US Navy from the year 1797. Some sites require admission. The round trip take three to four hours. Tip: begin at the *Boston Common State House*. Orientation maps are available at the *Boston Common Visitor Information Booth (Tremont St., near MBTA-Station Park St.).*

John Hancock Observatory (U/B6)
From the 60th floor of this skyscraper built by the architect I. M. Pei, the tallest structure in New England, you have a bird's eye view of Boston. *Trinity Pl./ St. James Ave.; Mon–Sat 9 am– 10 pm, Sun 9 am–5 pm; admission $1; Tel. 617/572 64 29*

New England Aquarium (U/F4)
More than 2,000 different marine creatures. Visitors descend into a large pool via a glass staircase among sharks and morays without so much as getting their feet wet. *Central Wharf (Central/ Milk St.), 1 Atlantic Ave.; Mon–Fri 9 am–5 pm, Sat, Sun, 9 am–6 pm; admission $12; Tel. 617/973 52 00*

MUSEUMS

Boston Tea Party Ship and Museum (U/F5)
On board the *"Beaver II"* the historical *Tea Party* is re-enacted daily; in protest against the British tariffs levied on tea, the bales went swimming. *Congress St. Bridge; daily 9 am–5 pm; admission $8; Tel. 617/338 17 73*

The Computer Museum (U/F5)
The only museum in the world exclusively devoted to computer technology. Kids will also find a tour through the 15x larger-than-life-sized model of a PC. *300 Congress St.; Tues–Sun 10 am– 6 pm; winter 10 am–5 pm; admission $7; Tel. 617/426 28 00*

Isabella Stewart Gardner Museum (O)
Museum in the one-time personal palazzo of a female millionaire with exquisite old masters (Botticelli, Rubens, Tizian)

as well as Medici treasures. *280 The Fenway; Tues–Sun 11 am–5 pm; admission $10; weekends $11; Tel. 617/566 14 01*

John F. Kennedy Library and Museum (O)

Mementoes from the period in office of the 35th president of the US, born in Boston and assassinated in Dallas in 1963. Before the bold, black glass building of the architect I.M. Pei, Kennedy's sailing yacht in dry-dock can be viewed, "Victura". *Columbia Point, Dorchester; Subway Station JFK/U Mass (Red Line); daily 9 am–5 pm; admission $8; Tel. 617/929 45 23*

Museum of Fine Arts (O)

One of the most renowned art museums in the country. It offers, among other things, a generous overview of the artistic endeavour in the US. The Asiatic Collection is considered particularly profound. Likewise recommended: the Egyptian Section, the Indian miniatures, the Impressionists, the *gift shop* with copies of old jewellery and other artful souvenirs as well as a good restaurant. For culture vultures, a must. *465 Huntington Ave.; daily 10 am till 4.45 pm; Wed until 9.45 pm; admission $10; Tel. 617/267 93 00*

"USS Constitution" (U/E1)

The 200-year-old metal vessel engaged in 42 sea battles – and won them all. Museum with photos, paintings and sailors' equipment. *Constitution Wharf, Charlestown, approach by water shuttle boat ($1) from Long Wharf next to the New England Aquarium; in summer daily 9 am–6 pm; admission voluntary; Tel. 617/426 18 12*

RESTAURANTS

Anthony's Pier 4 (U/F4–5)

Homemade, marinated salmon, cod and lobster of the finest sort. Meeting place: the bar called *Rum Room. 140 Northern Ave.; Tel. 617/ 482 62 62; category 1*

In memory of the most famous Bostonian of all: the John F. Kennedy Library

Biba's (U/C5)

Lydia Shire is one of the most innovative of America's culinary talents. *272 Boylston St.; Tel. 617/426 78 78, category 1*

Brasserie Jo (U/A6)

A Frenchman interprets the *smaller denizens of the sea's bottom* with American fish nobility and serves great *choucroute* (pickled cabbage). *In the Colonnade Hotel, 120 Huntington Ave.; Tel. 617/425 32 40; category 2*

Clio (O)

Kitchen chef Ken Oringer serves up innovative creations such as foie gras with rhubarb and figs or kid. *In the Eliot Hotel, 370 Commonwealth Ave.; Tel. 617/536 72 00; category 1*

Hamersley's Bistro (O)

Innovative New England dishes in the trendy South End quarter. *553 Tremont St.; Tel. 617/423 27 00; category 1*

Jimmy's Harborside (O)

⚘ Fish with 🔆 view to the harbour. The Boat Bar is where the local political crew gets together. *242 Northern Ave.; Tel. 617/423 10 00; category 2*

Joe's American Bar & Grill (U/F3)

Lively meeting spot for seafood and steak. 🔆 Nice harbour view from the terrace. *100 Atlantic Ave.; Tel. 617/367 87 00; category 2*

Legal Sea Food (U/C5)

Popular fish restaurant with offshoots on Copley Square, in Cambridge and at Logan Airport. *35 Columbus Ave.; Tel. 617/426 44 44; category 3*

Mistral (U/B–C6)

In this one-time bicycle factory Mediterranean seafood makes up the bill of fare. *223 Columbus Ave.; Tel. 617/867 93 00; category 2*

Olives (O)

Chief cook Todd English offers variations on an imaginative Mediterranean kitchen. He is also proprietor of the four *Figs*-restaurants in Boston – always good for a snack *(category 3). 10 City Square, Charlestown; Tel. 617/242 19 99; category 2*

Radius (U/E5)

Here's where Michael Schlow, a new star in the culinary heavens, does his thing. The menu offers fresh delicacies such as Jacob's oysters from Maine with forest mushrooms. Reserve far in advance! *8 High St.; Tel. 617/426 12 34; category 1*

Union Oyster House (U/E3)

At the bar of the oldest restaurants in the city one enjoys fresh Blue-Point oysters. *41 Union St.; Tel. 617/227 27 50; category 2*

Charles Street (U/C4)

At the foot of Beacon Hill antique dealers are right at home. Good deals amid mountains of junk is the promise of the *Beacon Hill Thrift Shop (15 Charles St.).*

Faneuil Hall Marketplace (U/E3)

Once the largest markets in the city has meanwhile become a Mecca for the "buying kind" of tourists. Good restaurants are also found here, among them *Marketplace Café,* the *Durgin Park*

44

and the *Quincy Market* in a historical market structure from the year 1825. ⚡❖ In the evenings the bars are meeting places for singles and seekers.

Filene's Basement   (U/D4)
In this forerunner of the "outlet stores" one can always discover respectable bargains from the fabrication of well-known fashion trend-setters. *426 Washington St.; Tel. 617/542 20 11*

Newbury Street   (U/A–C 6–5)
Boston's major business artery extends over 12 blocks from Common to the west through the Back Bay district and offers big-city department-store atmosphere and oftentimes boutique charm.

HOTELS

Boston Harbor   (U/F4)
On the water, with spectacular ◀↓▶ view over city and harbour. Good fitness club. *230 rooms; 70 Rowes Wharf, Boston; Tel. 617/439 70 00; Fax 330 94 50; category 1*

Chandler Inn   (U/B–C6)
Simple house with 56 smaller rooms in close proximity to Back Bay. Good base camp for exploring the city on foot. *26 Chandler St., Boston; Tel. 617/482 34 50; Fax 542 34 28; category 2*

Lenox   (U/A6)
House dating from the turn of the century in Back Bay. Always ask about *special rates. 214 rooms; 710 Boylston St., Boston; Tel. 617/536 53 00; Fax 267 12 37; category 2*

The Newbury Guest House   (U/A6)
15 rooms in a renovated house near Copley Square. *261 Newbury St., Boston; Tel. 617/ 437 76 66; Fax 262 42 43; category 2–3*

Hotel rooms at reduced rates sold by *Hotel Reservations Network (Tel. 214/361 73 11; Fax 361 72 99)* and *Quikbook (Tel. 212/532 16 60; Fax 532 15 56).*

Private accommodations from $ 80 to $250 available from *Bed & Breakfast Agency of Boston (47 Commercial Wharf, Boston; Tel. 617/720 35 40; Fax 523 57 61).* You can also book by Internet: *www.boston-bnagency. com.*

Between $70 and $200 is the going price for rooms at *B & B Reservation Service (P.O. Box 600035, Newtonville; Tel. 617/964 16 06; Fax 332 85 72),* which also offers rooms in other parts of Massachusetts. On the website *www.bbre-serve.com* you can obtain an idea; still, booking must be done via the agency.

SPORTS & LEISURE

Cycling   (U/A–C 5–1)
Tip: the 30-km-long *Dr. Paul Dudley White Bikeway* on both sides of the Charles River.

ENTERTAINMENT

The *Calendar* in the Thursday edition of the *Boston Globe*, the weekly *Boston Phoenix* and the monthly city newspaper *Boston Magazine* contain up-to-date info on what's afoot in the cultural scene.

Bar   (U/C4)
Bull and Finch Pub. Interiour and atmosphere like Old England. *84 Beacon St.; Tel. 617/227 96 05*

Live music (O)

The *Lansdowne St.* between *Brook-line Ave.* and *Ipswich St. (MBTA Green Line: Kenmore Sq.)* is full of live music. Among others in the discothèques *Axis (Tel. 617/626 24 37)* and *Avalon (Tel. 617/262 24 24)* and in Mama Kin *(Tel. 617/536 21 00)* you can listen to the Boston band Aerosmith.

Symphony Hall (O)

Home of the Boston Symphony Orchestra and the beloved Boston Pop Orchestra. *301 Massachusetts Ave.: Tel. 617/266 14 92*

INFORMATION

Greater Boston Convention and Visitors Bureau (U/A6)

Prudential Tower, Centre Court, 800 Boylston St.; Mon–Fri 8.30 am–6 pm, Sat, Sun 10 am–6 pm; Tel. 617/536 41 00; www.bostonusa.com

Information Booth (U/D4)

Here's where to pick up cards for the Freedom Trail. *Northeast corner of the Boston Common (Tremont St.)*

CAMBRIDGE

(109/E2) ★ Dyed-in-the-wool Bostonians consider Cambridge a part of their city; the residents of Cambridge itself, however, do not agree. The politically independent community on the northern side of the Charles River, reachable by MBTA (Red Line), is the location of *Harvard University.*

🏃⚛ Harvard Square is the centre of the city. There one meets students, strolls through the boutiques, which still exude the aroma of the 1960s, visits cafés, bookshops and health food stores with organic items.

Cambridge is a contemplative starting point for a visit to Boston. Recommended is the round trip with the *Old Town Trolley (departure: Harvard Square).*

The young Internet crowd congregates in 🏃 *Café Cybersmith (36 Church St.).* The most attractive meeting spot later in the evening: 🏃 *House of Blues (96 Winthrop St.; Tel. 617/491 25 83)* live music and young people everywhere.

RESTAURANT

East Coast Grill

Lively scene, meeting place with grill specialities and good fish dishes. *271 Cambridge St.; Tel. 617/491 65 68; category 2*

HOTELS

Charles

A serene oasis amid the hubbub of Harvard Square. Among the plus points of the establishment is the Regatta Bar, one of the best jazz bars in the region. *340 rooms; 1 Bennett St., Cambridge; Tel. 617/864 12 00; Fax 864 57 15; category 1*

Susse Chalet Inn

Motel in an industrial district about a ten-minute drive north of Harvard Square. Plus point: rooms starting from $99. *211 Concord Turnpike; Tel. 617/661 78 00; Fax 868 81 53; category 2–3*

CAPE COD

(109/E-F 3–4) ★ The peninsula lies east of Boston and looks like an

Relaxation pure and simple on the beach at Cape Cod

arm with flexed muscle. Exactly inside the fist is *Provincetown*, where the Pilgrims dropped anchor from the "Mayflower" in 1620, before sailing on to Plymouth. In the 17th century, fishermen settled here and shipped salted mackerels and cod as far as southern Europe.

The Cape, with its shady core, covered with thick woods and cranberry fields, rimmed by broad, sandy beaches lured rich Bostonians, artists and writers. Three and one half million tourists come calling during the summer months between June and September. The most obvious effects of this deluge: row upon row of motels and supermarkets along the main thorough streets, traffic jams and back-ups on the bridges and along Route 6. And still, the 500 kilometres of coastline with their old wooden houses and fishing villages as well as the villas of the rich and the pleasant sea breeze all conspire to mediate a feeling of holiday and the aura of an insider tip. Three

bridges, erected in 1914, transverse the old canal from "the continent" to Cape Cod, divided into the districts North Cape (from Sandwich to Orleans), South Cape (from Falmouth to Chatham) and Outer Cape (the remaining portion up to Provincetown).

On Route 28 one reaches *Falmouth*, where several old houses surround the town's public park *(info: Falmouth Historical Society; Palmer Ave.; Tel. 508/548 48 57)*. To the south lies *Woods Hole*, departure point for the ferry to *Martha's Vineyard* and *Nantucket*, to the east is *Hyannis*. In the harbour suburb Hyannisport, concealed behind thick hedges is the summer seat of the Kennedy family. For the best view, take to the water – i.e., a harbour roundtrip *(Hy-Line, Ocean St. Dock; Tel. 508/778 26 00)*. An alternative: a visit to the *John F. Kennedy Hyannis Museum (379 Main St.; Tel. 508/790 30 77)*.

Via Route 28 one reaches travelling eastward a picturesque spot *Chatham*, where a water taxi is available to the beaches of *South* and *North Beach Island* as well as to *National Wildlife Refuge Monomoy Island.*

Route 6 takes one to 🚶 *Provincetown*, an artists colony and traditional meeting place for thousands of gays from the northeastern US. There one also finds the tower of the 🔖 *Pilgrim Monument*, a granite copy of the Torre del Mangia in Siena *(High Pole Hill/Winslow St.; Tel. 508/487 13 10)*, from whose top one can almost survey the entire Cape. The neighbouring *Provincetown Museum* shows the captain's cabin of a whaling boat.

The tiny community of ==Wellfleet== (halfway between Orleans and Provincetown), offers a welcome contrast to the Cod commotion. Most Cape oysters come from Wellfleet ==oyster banks.== Entertainment of a completely different kind is offered by ==one of the last surviving drive-in cinemas in the country.== *(Route 6; Tel. 508/349 71 76).* North-Cape attractions are *Brewster* on Route 6 A, *Yarmouthport* and *Barnstable*, where some of the island's prettiest inns and restaurants are to be found. The core of *Sandwich*, the oldest settlement on the Cape, dates back to the year 1639. The oldest building, the *Hoxie House (Water St.; Route 130)*, displays old daily-use furniture from the Founders' Period. The *Sandwich Glass Museum*, previously a glass factory *(Town Hall Square; Tel. 508/888 02 51)*, and the *Yesteryears Museum* with two floors full of puppets and their accoutrements *(River St./Main St.; Tel. 508/888 17 11)* are two additional attractions.

Aesop's Table

Here one finds fish combined with the very best from the vegetable garden. *Main St., Wellfleet; Tel. 508/349 64 50; category 2*

Chillingsworth

French cuisine and an excellent wine card in a 300-year-old Cape house. *Main St., Brewster; Tel. 508/896 36 40; category 2*

Daniel Webster Inn

In the cosy *tavern* fish specialities taste the best. *149 Main St., Sandwich; Tel. 508/888 36 22; category 1–2*

Front Street

Bistro of the best sort. Specialities lamb. *230 Commercial St., Provincetown; Tel. 508/487 9715; category 2*

The Impudent Oyster

Fish dishes and clams. *15 Chatham Bars Ave., Chatham; Tel. 508/945 35 45; category 2*

Bed & Breakfast Cape Cod

Photos of accommodations between $75 and $200 can be viewed beforehand on the Internet: *www.bedandbreakfastcapecod.com.* To book, however, contact the office directly by telephone or fax. *Box 341, Hyannisport; Tel. 508/775 27 72; Fax 240 05 99*

Captain Ferris

Beautifully renovated old house. *12 rooms, 308 Old Main St., South Yarmouth; Tel. 508/760 28 18; Fax 398 12 62; category 1–2*

Chatham Bars Inn
Hotel with private beach and pools. *205 rooms; Shore Rd., Chatham; Tel. 508/945 00 96; Fax 945 54 91; category 1*

The Inn at Duck Creek
One-time captain's house. *25 rooms, East Main St., Wellfleet; Tel. 508/349 93 33; Fax 349 02 34; category 3*

Land's End Inn
One-time tradesman's house. *17 rooms; 22 Commercial St., Province-town; Tel. 508/487 07 06; no fax, category 1–3*

The Queen Anne Inn
Pretty old thing. *31 rooms; 70 Queen Anne Rd., Chatham; Tel. 508/945 03 94; Fax 945 48 84; category 1*

Watermark Inn
Ten suites off the tourist track with built-in kitchens and a wonderful view to the water. *603 Commercial St., Provincetown; Tel. 508/255 06 17; Fax 240 00 17; category 1–2*

SPORTS & LEISURE

Boats
Motor- and sailboats can be rented in every harbour, among others from *Flyer's (131 A Commercial St., Provincetown; Tel. 508/487 08 98).*

Bicycles
Cape Cod is criss-crossed by cycling paths. Recommended are the *Cape Cod Rail Trail* (from Dennis to Eastham) and the *Provincelands Trail* (it runs through the area of the Cape Cod National Seashore).

Beaches
The *Cape Cod National Seashore* on the northwest coast between Chatham and Provincetown offers splendid sand, cliffs, dunes, moor landscape, bike and hiking paths. *Cape Cod National Seashore Headquarters; Route 6; Eastham; Tel. 508/255 34 21*

Whale Watching
From the middle of April to Oct. the whales tumble about before the *Stellwagen Bank* 15 km east of Provincetown. The giant sea mammals are an impressive sight. *Dolphin Fleet, MacMillan Pier; Tel. 508/349 19 00*

Hiking
The *Massachusetts Audubon Society* offers among other things tips for trips to the *National Wildlife Refuge Monomoy Island,* an island cut into by an enormous tidal wave; the island is home to rare deer, reptiles and birds. *South Wellfleet; Tel. 508/349 26 15*

INFORMATION

Cape Cod Information Booth
In the most important places on the Cape *Information stands are open from Memorial Day to Labor Day.*

Cape Cod Chamber of Commerce
Route 6/Route 132, Hyannis; Tel. 508/362 32 25; Mon–Fri 8.30 am– 5 pm, in the summer also Sat, Sun 10 am–4 pm

DEERFIELD

(108/C3) Twice in the 18th century this village in the valley of the Connecticut River, called Pioneer Valley, was overrun by hostile Indians. Today Main Street is a good example of the different architectural style for the period between the 18th and 20th centuries.

Historic Deerfield
The Street (Route 5/Route 10), via Exit 24 north of the I-91; daily 9.30 am–4.30 pm; admission $12; Tel. 413/774 55 81

Deerfield Inn
In a historical building. The restaurant serves dishes according to recipes found in the library of the town. *23 rooms; The Street, Deerfield; Tel. 413/774 55 87; Fax 773 87 12; category 1*

GLOUCESTER

(**109/E2**) In his European bestseller *The Storm* Sebastian Junger described the sinking of a fishing boat from this harbour town in a frightful "nor'easter", the storms that come up from the north east. Today, as well, one lives in this village founded in 1623, from the harvest of the sea. Local renown: restaurants that serve the catch on the same day it was hauled on board, those on Main Street and the Seven Seas Wharf. Gloucester is only 20 km from the *Stellwagen Bank*, the feeding site of whales, sharks and dolphins.

Woodman's
❖ Simple place near Crane Beach with outstanding lobster and local specialities *clambake* (different frutti di mare, "corn on the cob"). *126 Main St., Essex; Tel. 978/768 60 57; category 3*

The galleries, studios and shops of *Rocky Neck* (right next to Main St.) always have something for the art devotee.

Vista Motel
Motel with ✺ view of the harbour. Pool. *40 rooms; 22 Thatcher Rd., Gloucester; Tel. 978/281 34 10; no fax; category 2–3*

Observing Whales
The best time is early morning. Trips are undertaken by *Cape Ann Whale Watch (415 Main St.; Tel. 978/283 51 10); Captain Billy's Whale Watch (33 Harbor Loop; Tel. 978/283 69 95)* and *Yankee Fleet (75 Essex Ave.; Tel. 978/283 03 13).*

Cape Ann Chamber of Commerce
33 Commercial St.; Tel. 978/283 16 01; Mon–Fri 8 am–5 pm

Rockport   (**109/E2**)
Not to be missed is a trip via ★ Route 127 A to *Rockport* at the point of Cape Ann. The *galleries* on Bearskin Neck testify to the town's past as an artist colony. In a wooden cabin *Lobster Pool (329 Granite St.; Tel. 978/546 78 08; category 3)* serves tasty fish. The town boasts an entire series of

pleasant historical inns. Overnight stays with a view 🌊 to the sea at *Yankee Clipper Inn (26 rooms; 96 Granite St.; Tel. 978/546 34 07; Fax 546 97 30; category 1–2)*.

GREAT BARRINGTON

(108/B3) The wooded Berkshire Mountains in the west are listed among visitors' travel favourites not only in the autumn when the leaves begin to change. Great Barrington, the first city in the world in which electrical street lighting was installed (1886), *Southfield* and *New Marlborough* (in the summer its own music festival), likewise in the neighbouring *South Egremont and Sheffield* are rewarding places to visit in the summer months, especially valued by antique collectors and culture devotees.

RESTAURANT

The Old Mill
Dinner in an old mill. *53 Main St. (Route 23); South Egremont; Tel. 413/528 14 21; category 2*

SHOPPING

The Buggy Whip Factory
In a one-time whip factory more than 95 antique dealers have opened shop and the *Cottage Cafe*, a restaurant with good sandwiches. *Route 272; Southfield; Tel. 413/229 35 76*

HOTEL

Old Inn on the Green
A house from the year 1760 with 15 rooms and two suites. First-class restaurant. *Route 57;* *New Marlborough; Tel. 413/229 31 31; Fax 229 82 36; category 1*

INFORMATION

Southern Berkshires Chamber of Commerce
362 Main St.; Mon–Fri 9.30 am–4.30 pm; Sat–4.30 pm; Tel. 413/528 15 10

LENOX

(108/B3) Between the end of June and September is the charming wooded landscape of the ★ Berkshires with its soft hills and shining lakes the showplace for America's most renowned ◆ *Open-Air Music Festival* in *Tanglewood.* Houses and parks are the summer residence of the Boston Symphony Orchestra. One picnics and listens to the concerts of well-known guest celebrities. Besides the works of classical music, Tanglewood also boasts superb jazz on its program. Nearby: the Shopping Outlet Center Lee (via Route 20).

SIGHTS

Gilded Age Cottages
Around the turn of the last century, the Berkshires near Newport (Rhode Island) and the Adirondacks in New York State were the areas in which rich New Yorkers and Bostonians built the spacious summer houses, called with gracing modesty *cottages.* Open to the public are, for example, *Naumkeag (Tel. 413/298 32 39); Chesterwood (Tel. 413/298 35 79)* and *The Mount (Tel. 413/637 18 99),* the house of the author Edith Wharton.

Norman Rockwell Museum

Here on display are 150 drawings of the famous newspaper illustrator Norman Rockwell (1894–1978), among them his humorous cover pictures for the magazine *Saturday Evening Post. Route 183; Stockbridge; daily 10 am–5 pm; admission $9; Tel. 413/298 41 00*

Blantyre

This one-time cottage with numerous Gothic towers is today a luxurious inn with a good restaurant. *Route 20; Tel. 413/637 35 56; category 1*

Wheatleigh

This summer residence, inspired by Italy, has a magnificent view ⚜ of the Stockbridge Bowl. Today a luxurious inn with exquisite kitchen. *Hawthorne Rd.; Tel. 413/637 06 10, category 1*

Brook Farm Inn

Country farmhouse. Six of the 12 rooms have a fireplace. *15 Hawthorne St., Lenox; Tel. 413/637 30 13; Fax 637 47 51; category 1–2*

Canyon Ranch

Luxury fitness holidays on the grounds of a castle. *120 rooms; 165 Kemble St., Lenox; Tel. 413/637 41 00, Fax 637 00 57; category 1*

The Village Inn

Simple inn in the town centre. *32 rooms; 16 Church St., Lenox; Tel. 413/637 00 20; Fax 637 97 56; category 1–2*

Lenox Chamber of Commerce

65 Main St.; Mon–Fri 10 am–4 pm, in the summer also Sat 10 am–6 pm and Sun 11 am–2 pm; Tel. 413/637 36 46
Information on Tanglewood: Tel. 413/637 61 80

MARTHA'S VINEYARD

(109/E4) ★ In 1660 a Boston tradesman named Mayhew bought an island 330 sq km in area which reminds visitors of the Irish coast. His sons were missionaries to the Wampanoag Indians, whose descendants are still residents in *Gay Head* on the western end of the island. The rest of the island has meanwhile become the chosen spot for the weekend and summer domicile of prominent people. The memories of the Christian movement and whaling only populate the heads of romantics today. *Vineyard Haven*, where the ferries from Woods Hole and Hyannis put in, has remained a sleepy nest. *Oak Bluffs* on the other hand has become commercialized to a great degree. The Victorian cottages in the town centre are worth a look. The perfect holiday retreat is, however, *Edgartown.* Before its coast lies an infamous island, reachable by ferry, *Chappaquiddick.* In *West Tisbury* and *Chilmark* there are small restaurants offering a pleasant and enjoyable half-time break on the cycling tour to Gay Head. The granite cliffs of Gay Head rear up some 50 m above the surf and shimmer in all the hues of red and blue. Nudist bathing, otherwise strictly forbidden, is a matter of course here. Not only at sundown does the cliff at the western end offer a  marvellous view. *By car you can travel to Woods Hole by ferry (Steamship Authority; Tel. 508/228 32 74), as passenger or cyclist also from Hyannis (Hy-Line Cruises; Tel. 508/778 26 00) or from New Bedford (Cape Island Express Line; Tel. 508/997 16 88). In the summer and on weekends you are well advised to reserve a space for your car as early as possible!*

Martha's Vineyard – a must

RESTAURANTS

Only in Edgartown and Oak Bluffs is alcohol served in restaurants. In other places you must bring it with you. The bottles are opened (often for a small charge = *corkage fee*).

Beach Plum Inn
Great Lobster, good duck. *Beach Plum Lane, Menemsha; Tel. 508/645 94 54; category 1–2*

Home Port
Simple house, fresh fish. Even more reasonable: order the food at the take-out counter and enjoy on benches in front of the house. *North Rd., Menemsha; Tel. 508/645 26 79; category 2*

The Red Cat
Her tuna fish and steak top the list. For that reason: reserve at all costs! *688 State Rd., West Tisbury; Tel. 508/693 95 99; category 1*

SHOPPING

Old antique shops, galleries and boutiques are to be found in Edgartown. Popular: the flea market in *Chilmark (Wed and Sat, both days in the morning).*

HOTELS

Admiral Benbow Inn
Bed & Breakfast with a veranda typical for New England . *7 pleasant rooms; 520 New York Ave., Oak Bluffs; Tel. 508/693 68 25; Fax 696 61 91; category 1–2*

Charlotte Inn
Formerly the house of a whaling fleet owner. The 23 rooms are decorated with antiques. *27 S Summer St., Edgartown; Tel. 508/627 47 51; Fax 627 46 52; category 1*

The Farmhouse B & B
Five rooms in a cosy farm house. *State Rd., North Tisbury; Tel. 508/693 53 54; Fax 693 54 98; category 1*

The Inn at Blueberry Hill
Luxurios house among green fields. In the building of the restaurant *Theo's. North Rd., Chilmark; Tel. 508/645 33 22; category 1*

Lambert's Cove Country Inn
An old farmhouse set in an apple orchard. Outstanding restaurant.

15 rooms; Lambert's Cove Rd., West
Tisbury; Tel. 508/693 22 98; Fax
693 78 90; category 1–2

Menemsha Inn and Cottages
Located in a quiet part of the island. 15 rooms and 12 Cottages;
North Rd., Menemsha; Tel. 508/
645 25 21; no fax; category 1–2

HOUSES/BED & BREAKFAST

Rooms located and rented by
Martha's Vineyard and Nantucket
Reservations (Vineyard Haven; Tel.
508/693 72 00, no fax).
   Rental of beautifully located
apartments or single houses are
available through Barbara Nevin
Real Estate (Edgartown; Tel.
508/627 71 77; Fax 627 71 79)
and Ocean Park Realty (Oak
Bluffs; Tel. 508/693 42 10; Fax
693 89 92).

SPORTS & LEASURE

Bicycles
Rental: R.W. Cutler Bike, Edgartown (Tel. 508/627 40 52)

Golf
Members of other clubs can also
play on the green of Farm
Neck Golf Club (18 holes; Tel.
508/693 25 04) in Oak Bluffs
(Greenfee $75).

Beaches
East Beach on Chappaquidis is
crowded even on a day when
few people arrive. The South
Beach is recommended to
surfers. For the car you need a
parking ID, which is made available among other services in the
hotel. Cheaper and more eco-
logically friendly: arriving by
bike.

INFORMATION

Martha's Vineyard
Chamber of Commerce
Beach Rd., Vineyard Haven; Tel.
508/693 00 85; Mon–Fri 9 am–
5 pm, also in the summer daily
8 am–8 pm at the ferry terminal

NANTUCKET

(109/F4) ★ Nantucket, only about
one half as large as the neighbouring Martha's Vineyard, is
twice as far from the mainland.
The name means "distant island"
in Indian language. The location
alone makes the island a gem. In
July and September one finds an
island upon which time seems to
have stood still. It must have
been sometime back in the 19th
century when Nantucket was
the most important whaling port
in the world and the ideal showplace for the novel Moby Dick,
written by the New Englander
Herman Melville.
   Besides the endless landscape
of dunes, beach and moor, typical for the island's image are
the weather-proofed wooden
houses with their shingle-roofs.
   The ferry from Hyannis at
Cape Cod sets over to Nantucket: Steamship Authority, Tel.
508/477 86 00. In the summer
it's not terribly easy to secure a
space for your car. The wisest
thing is to park the car on the
mainland and just ride over as a
regular passenger.

MUSEUM

Whaling Museum
In formers times a factory in
which sperm oil was processed.
Now an exhibition hall for the

Away from it all among the dunes on Nantucket

achievements of the whaling business. *Steamboat Wharf/ Broad St.; in the summer daily 10 am–5 pm, in the winter Sat, Sun 11 am–1 pm; admission $5; Tel. 508/228 18 94*

RESTAURANTS

American Seasons
Creative US-specialities are served. *80 Center St.; April–Dec; Tel. 508/228 71 11; category 2*

The Brant Point Grill
Fish from the grill served directly at the water. *White Elephant Resort; Easton Rd.; Tel. 508/228 25 00; category 1–2*

Brotherhood of Thieves
● Pleasant pub, in which however no credit cards are accepted and which refuses to give its telephone number. *23 Broad St.; category 3*

Seagrill
Lively fish restaurant with attractive prices. *45 Sparks Ave.; Tel. 508/325 57 00; category 2–3*

SHOPPING

Lightship Baskets
According to local tradition, the women of Nantucket carry baskets with artfully decorated covers as handbags. The most beautiful examples are to be found at *Four Winds Craft Guild* at *Ray's Court.*

HOTELS

Brant Point Inn/ Atlantic Mainstay
Two inns with quite spacious rooms. *17 rooms; 2 suites; 6 North Beach St., Nantucket; Tel. 508/228 54 42; Fax 228 84 98; category 2*

Brass Lantern Inn
The house in the historical quarter of the downtown lies, with its prices, at the lower end of the expensive scale. *17 rooms; 11 Water St., Nantucket; Tel. 508/228 40 64; Fax 325 09 28; category 1–2*

76 Main Street
Bed & Breakfast in the middle of town and yet, a few of the 18

rooms are located in a motel annex. *76 Main St., Nantucket; Tel. and Fax 508/228 25 33; category 1–2*

The Wauwinet
Luxurious inn with 29 rooms and five cottages, elegantly furnished. View to the sea. Tennis, water sport, restaurant *Topper's. Wauwinet Rd., Nantucket; Tel. 508/228 01 45; Fax 228 67 12; category 1*

Cycles
The number-one choice for locomotion can be rented from *Young's Bicycle Shop; Steamboat Wharf; Tel. 508/228 11 51.*

Beaches
❂ *Surfside* is the often frequented playground of surfers, *Madaket* and *Siaskonset* are, on the contrary, more secluded places.

Nantucket Chamber of Commerce
48 Main St., Nantucket; Mon–Fri 9 am–5 pm; Tel. 508/228 17 00

NEW BEDFORD

(109/E4) Some of the old patricians' houses in the harbour town near Rhode Island have been well tended to and are in good condition. Galleries, boutiques and restaurants have moved into the former business quarters of the fishing industry, giving the area an eclectic feeling. Outlet stores dominate the picture in business life.

New Bedford Whaling Museum
The house is dedicated to the 200-year history of whaling in the region. *18 Johnny Cake Hill; daily 9 am–5 pm; admission: $4.50; Tel. 508/997 00 46*

Antonio's
Here's where to try out the old recipes of the Portugese immigrants. *267 Coggeshall St.; Tel. 508/990 36 36; category 3*

Freestones
Enjoy good steaks in the centre of New Bedford's historical quarter. *41 William St.; Tel. 508/993 74 77; category 3*

Seaport Inn
Motel directly at the harbour (ferry to Martha's Vineyard). *94 rooms; 110 Middle St., Fairhaven; Tel. 997 12 88; Fax 996 57 27; category 2–3*

New Bedford Visitors Center
33 Williams St.; daily 9 am–4 pm; Tel. 508/991 62 00

PITTSFIELD

(108/B3) In the industrial centre of West Massachusetts lies the concentration of the paper industry. South of the city on Route 7 lies *Arrowhead*, the house in which the author Herman Melville penned his masterpiece *Moby Dick (780 Holmes Rd.; Tel. 413/442 17 93).*

The face of Plymouth – Justice guards over New England

MUSEUM

Hancock Shaker Village

★ An open-air museum laid out in grand style, 20 buildings remain, which documents architecture, style of living, tool making and gardening of the strict Quaker sect. 300 members of the religious community lived in this village in the 1830s, as abstinent as monks in a monastery. A masterpiece of functional design is the circular 3-storey stone stall in which one man would feed 54 cows at the same time. The village was transformed into a museum in the 1930s due to falling membership in the sect. Simple restaurant, gift boutique. *Route 20, 8 km west of Pittsfield; open from the end of May until the middle of Oct.; daily 9.30 am–5 pm; admission $12.50; Tel. 413/443 01 88*

HOTELS

Hancock Inn

Simple down-home accommodations where a good dinner is offered – in the summer Friday through Sunday. *6 rooms; 102*

Main St., Hancock; Tel. 413/738 58 73; Fax 738 57 19; category 3

Old Chatham Sheepherding Company Inn

The small house set out in the country has nine rooms and a great restaurant. *99 Shaker Museum Rd., Old Chatham; Tel. 518/794 97 74; Fax 794 97 79; cate-gory 1*

INFORMATION

Berkshire Visitors Bureau

Berkshire Commons in the Crowne Plaza Complex, Pittsfield; Mon–Fri 8.30 am–4 pm; Tel. 413/443 91 86

PLYMOUTH

(109/E3) Plymouth Rock, the very spot at which the Pilgrim Fathers of the "Mayflower" 1620 went ashore in search of the already established colony Virginia, rests today under a neoclassical monument from the year 1880. *Pilgrim Path*, a foot trail running along numerous historical sites, leads to a faithfully reproduced replica, the

Replica of the "Mayflower", with which the Pilgrims crossed the ocean

"Mayflower II", which was incidentally launched and really stays afloat.

Plymouth (36,000 inhabitants) is the self-styled capital of cranberry cultivation. Information between April and November: *Cranberry World Visitors Center; 225 Water St.; Tel. 508/747 23 50.* The harvest in October creates a particularly picturesque mood.

MUSEUMS

Pilgrim Hall Museum
Household utensils, weapons and books of the Pilgrim Fathers. *75 Court St./Route 3 A; daily 9.30 am–4.30 pm; admission $5; Tel. 508/746 16 20*

Plimouth Plantation
A museum village, in which the life of the early settlers is impressively and faithfully re-enacted. A visit is also worth making with the little ones.

Warren Ave./Route 3 A; 30 April–1 Dec.; daily 9 am–5 pm; admission $19; Tel. 508/746 16 22

RESTAURANT

Plymouth Bay Brewing Co.
American bistro-kitchen serves Golden Ale, brewed on location. *56 Main St. (Route 3 A); Tel. 508/746 72 22; category 2*

HOTEL

Pilgrim Sands Motel
Motel just opposite the Plimouth Plantation with its own small beach and two pools. *64 rooms; 150 Warren Ave.; Plymouth; Tel. 508/747 09 00; Fax 746 80 66; category 2*

INFORMATION

Destination Plymouth
225 Water St.; Mon–Fri 9 am–5 pm; Tel. 508/747 75 33

SALEM

(**109/E2**) Puritan mass hysteria in a small coastal village north of Boston led to a unique occurrence in America: the so-called witch trials, in the course of which 19 women were hanged. More than 200 were interrogated and tortured in the *Witch House (310 ¹/₂ Essex St.).* At the beginning of the 19th century Salem acquired a somewhat more pleasant reputation: here a spirited trade was carried on with the rest of the world. Ship builders, ship owners and captains built themselves houses with a grandiose view of the sea. Various buildings on Derby Street and Derby Wharf have been restored.

SIGHTS

House of the Seven Gables
A large garden complex with beautiful old buildings dating from the 17th century. *54 Turner St.; daily 10 am–5 pm (in summer longer); admission $7; Tel. 978/744 09 91*

MUSEUM

Peabody and Essex Museum
In the Peabody Museum you can admire treasures from trade with Asia carried on by the East India Marine Society. The three masters' houses, each dating from separate centuries and belonging to the Essex Institute, tell the fascinating history of the region. *East India Square; Mon–Sat 10 am–5 pm, Sun 12 am–5 pm; admission $8.50; Tel. 978/745 95 00*

RESTAURANT

Chase House
Enjoy your dinner in the middle of the harbour on a terrace. *Pickering Wharf; Tel. 978/744 00 00; category 2*

HOTEL

Hawthorne's
89 rooms and suites, furnished with old furniture. You can find it in the historical quarter. *On-The-Common, Salem; Tel. 978/744 40 80; Fax 745 98 42; category 1–2*

INFORMATION

Salem Chamber of Commerce
Old Town Hall, 32 Derby Square; Mon–Fri 9 am–5 pm; Tel. 978/744 00 04

SURROUNDING AREA

Marblehead   (109/E 2)
On the coast north of Boston well-heeled burghers erected their summer houses. Marblehead fell into disrepute among puritanical Bostonians due to the alleged drinking excesses practized there. Today the ambience presents a rather more charming face. Good fish to be had at *The Landing (81 Front St.; Tel. 781/631 18 78)* and the best fish soup at *The Barnacle (141 Front St.; Tel. 781/631 42 36).* Direct on the rocky cliff over the water lies the Victorian inn *Spray Cliff on the Ocean (7 rooms; 25 Spray Cliff; Tel. 781/631 67 89).* The trip to Marblehead is worthwhile alone because of the shops and galleries.

STURBRIDGE

(108/C3) Old Sturbridge Village is an artificial town with 40 old houses built in the various New England styles. Its aim is to capture the mood of 1830, when Sturbridge was the frontier to the Wild West. The atmosphere seems right in any case.

SIGHTS

Old Sturbridge Village
Route 20 (Exit 2 of the I-84); daily 9 am–5 pm; in winter 10 am–4 pm; admission $16; Tel. 508/347 33 62

HOTEL

Publick House Historic Inn
17 rooms with historical flair. In the restaurant you'll find simple but hearty New England fare. *Route 131; Sturbridge; Tel. 508/347 33 13; Fax 347 12 46; category 1–3*

Solitary life and love of freedom

Each year autumn is ablaze in New England's mountainous north

Beautiful white wooden houses and churches in small villages just as lovely, are surrounded by softly rolling green hills, which lent the state its original French name *Vermont*. The landscape signals a secluded romantic mood high in the north of New England. The once independent republic entered the Union of the 13 original states in 1791 as number 14. However, it was always careful to preserve its own individuality. The state between Canada, New York, New Hampshire and Massachusetts, with an area of 25,000 sq km, was the very first state to abolish slavery. Here hippies and other alternative thinkers have found, throughout the century, a starting point for genuine ecological pioneering.

Yet the short summers and harsh climate offer little opportunity for agricultral innovation. Milk, cheese, maple syrup and fruit have remained, for generations, the staples and

Indian Summer is at its most beautiful here. Then the leaves change colour

chief products of Vermont's economy. Thirty years ago New Yorkers discovered the sleepy strip of land and its 560,000 friendly inhabitants in four regions *Champlain Valley* in the west, *Green Mountains* in the middle, *Northeast Kingdom* in the upper right corner and the *Connecticut River Valley* in the southeast. The New Yorkers come primarily in the few weeks of *Indian Summer*, when the maple and birch leaves are transformed into a display resembling fireworks. But Vermont, whose ski slopes lie at 1,000 metres, has also made a name for itself as a winter-sports paradise.

The much higher and steeper *White Mountains* in *New Hampshire* are also a magnet for visitors. The state, which dunks its southeastern tip in the ocean 25 km long and whose most significant role is to provide the stage every four years for the first stop of presidential primary hopefuls, has always remained true to its conservative heritage. Local custom obliges one to care for one's belongings and protect them. Thus, it is logical that auto

61

MARCO POLO SELECTION: VERMONT AND NEW HAMPSHIRE

1 Brattleboro
Base for the Indian Summer in Vermont (page 63)

2 Canterbury Shaker Village
Character, Strictness, Style and Taste (page 65)

3 Mount Washington
The very best view of New England from its highest mountain (page 71)

4 Cycling:
Landscape for connoisseurs
Setting off from Manchester by bicycle (page 69)

5 Shelburne Museum
35 old houses and a prison of yesteryear (page 64)

6 Woodstock
The Rockefellers live in this small New England town (page 73)

"license plates" bear the proud slogan *Live free or die.*

The freedom that New Hampshire folks refer to is rooted in a grumpy, critical manner of viewing all forms of government. The around one million inhabitants live on 24,000 sq km and draw their living from processing industries and tourism. The 1,300 lakes as well as the mighty White Mountains with the towering Mount Washington (1,887 m) offer the perfect relief for those weary of the summer heat. 84 per cent of New Hampshire is covered with forests thanks to measures taken by Congress 80 years ago, "putting the law down" on lumberjacking and the like while acquiring 3,000 sq km of wooded areas now declared national forest preserves.

New Hampshire is divided geographically into six areas. From north to south, one has the *White Mountains, Dartmouth Lake Sunapee* and *Monadnock.* To the west on the border of Vermont, *Lake Country* borders Maine; *Merrimack Valley* with the capital Concord and the region *Seacoast* with the harbour city Portsmouth sits on the Atlantic.

BENNINGTON

(106/A5) Bennington, Vermont's second largest city, and its 35,000 inhabitants owe a lot to the economic up-swing of the mills and the pottery industry at the end of the 19th century. However, politically the area was important much earlier. It was actually in the Catamount Tavern that the freedom fighter Ethan Allen organised the Green Mountain Boys in 1775. Two years later General John Stark led them to war in the Battle for Independence against the British, themselves supported by numerous mercenary contingents from Germany, thence the old warning cry, "The Germans are coming!" The *Bennington Battle Monument*, a 100-metre-high obelisk recalls the victory *(15 Monument Ave.).*

Bennington Museum
In this museum one can have a look at household utensils, among them old pottery from Bennington, Tiffany glass and popular art. *West Main St./Route 9; daily 9 am–5 pm, in summer 9 am–6 pm; admission $6; Tel. 802/447 15 71*

Blue Benn
⚵ A typical diner in decor of the 1940s. Many college kids come here to enjoy hamburgers. *Route 7 N; Tel. 802/442 51 40; category 3*

Bennington Pottery
Pottery with a long tradition. Guided factory tour. *324 County St.; Tel. 802/447 75 31*

Best Western New Englander
Noble motel class. *58 rooms; 220 Northside Drive, Bennington; Tel. and Fax 802/442 63 11; category 2–3*

Bennington Area Chamber of Commerce
Veteran's Memorial Drive; Mon–Fri 9 am–5 pm, in the summer also Sat 9 am–5 pm and Sun 10 am–4 pm; Tel. 802/447 33 11

BRATTLEBORO

(106/B5) ★ The town in the southeast of Vermont with a population of 8,600 souls began as an outpost in "Indian country" and became in the 18th century an industry and recreation centre. The author Rudyard Kipling wrote his *Jungle Book* here. The excursion ship *"Belle of Brattleboro"* cruises in autumn on the Connecticut River and offers a spectacular view of the woods with their brilliant colours ◀▶ *(Tel. 802/254 12 63).*

The Latchis
Art-déco building. Many of the 30 rooms have a view to the river ◀▶. *50 Main St., Brattleboro, Tel. 802/254 63 00; Fax 254 63 04; category 3*

Kanu
The *Vermont Canoe Touring Center* arranges a 2-day raft tour. *Tel. 802/257 50 08*

Brattleboro Chamber of Commerce
180 Main St.; Mo–Fr 8.30 am–5 pm; Tel. 802/254 45 65

Marlboro *(106/C5)*
To the west 15 km lies the Marlboro College. In the summer the Marlboro Music Festival for Chamber Music takes place. In the autumn take in the New England Bach Festival. Overnight accommodations in the *Whetstone Inn Route 9;*

Tel. 802/254 25 00; which, in the 18th century, housed a tavern, post office and general store all in one.

BURLINGTON

(**106/A3**) The trading town on *Lake Champlain* grew up thanks to boat building and wood processing. Even today the business centre of Vermont has no more than 40,000 inhabitants and sits enthroned upon a hill above the sixth largest lake in the US. Burlington is seat of the University of Vermont, whose 10,000 students are impossible to overlook. Businesses and restaurants pepper Main Street and the shore promenade. Recommended: the pedestrian zone *Church Street Marketplace* and the restaurants *Sweet Tomatoes Trattoria* (pizza; *83 Church St.*), *Ice House* (fish; *171 Battery St.*) and *Isabel's on the Waterfront* (grill food and salads; *112 Lake St.*), all are category 2–3

MUSEUM

Shelburne Museum
★ Great effort was put forth to rescue 35 structures in various parts of New England. Here they are rebuilt and restored. Among them old bridges and a prison. *Route 7, Shelburne, 11 km south of Burlington; mid-May–Oct. daily 10 am–5 pm; admission $17.50; Tel. 802/985 33 44*

RESTAURANT

Cafe Shelburne
Bistro offers a respectable fish pot. *Route 7, Shelburne; closed afternoons and Mondays; Tel. 802/985 39 39, category 2*

HOTEL

The Inn at Shelburne Farms
Formerly summer palace. Many rooms have a great view ☙ to Lake Champlain. The restaurant, *The Dining Room,* is worth the wait. *24 rooms; Nov–May closed; Bay Rd./Harbor Rd., Shelburne; Tel. 802/985 84 98; Fax 985 12 33; category 1–2*

SPORTS & LEISURE

Kajak
Three- and four-day tours arranged by the inn *Paddle-Ways; P.O. Box 65125, Burlington; Tel. 802/660 86 06*

Cycling
Round trips, whereby luggage & equipment are seen to, can be arranged via several Vermont firms. E.g.: *Vermont Bicycle Touring; P.O. Box 711, Bristol, VT 05443; Tel 802/453 48 11*

INFORMATION

Lake Champlain Regional Chamber of Commerce
60 Main St.; Mon–Fri 8.30 am–5 pm, in the summer also Sat, Sun 11 am–3 pm; Tel. 802/863 34 89

SURROUNDING AREA

Lake Champlain (**106/A2–3**)
Lake Champlain stretches from the Canadian border 300 km southwards and joins Vermont with New York State. ☙ The lake has a breadth extending some 18 km which links, via the Champlain Channel, the Hudson with the Atlantic and, on the north, the St Lorenz Seaway. Ferries run between Charlotte (VT) and Essex (NY) likewise

Burlington *(Departure: King St. Dock; Tel. 802/864 98 04)* and Port Kent (NY). *Grand Isle* is the largest island in the lake. Route 2 leads from *Chimney Corner* to the mainland, Route 129 further to *Isle La Motte*, where, in 1666, Vermont's first settlement was established with Fort St Anne. The islands cast a special spell with a view to the 🍁 Green Mountains in the east and the densely wooded Adirondacks in the west. A pleasant overnight stay on the shore: *North Hero House* in *North Hero (26 rooms; Tel. 802/372 47 32; Fax 372 32 18; category 2–3)* and *Shore Acres Inn* at the same location *(23 rooms; Tel. 802/372 87 22; no fax; category 2–3).* Sports activities include swimming, sailing, canoeing, water-skiing and fishing.

CONCORD

(106/C5) New Hampshire, seat of government and the second-largest city in the state (pop. 35,800), lies in the valley of the Merrimack River. With great dignity the State House shimmers with its golden dome, ringed by monuments recalling the most important political leaders of the state. Concord's tribute to history stretches still further back. Here is where the first stage coaches that rumbled through the Wild West were built.

SIGHTS

Canterbury Shaker Village
★ Architecture, style of living and gardening in enchanting simplicity, just as the strictly religious Shaker sects preached in the 18th and 19th centuries. *288 Shaker Rd., Canterbury; May–Oct. daily 10 am–5 pm; admission $9.50; Tel. 603/783 95 11*

RESTAURANT

Creamery
New interpretations of old-time Shaker dishes. Fri and Sat dinner by candlelight. *Shaker Rd., Canterbury; reservations necessary; Tel. 603/783 95 11; category 2*

HOTEL

Ferry Point House
Victorian house on Lake Winnesquam, open only from May to the end of Oct. *7 rooms; 100 Lower Bay Rd., Sanbornton; Tel. 603/524 00 87; Fax 524 09 59; category 2–3*

On draught
How to tap maple trees, extract their sap and process it to syrup was all taught to the white settlers by the Indians. Today Vermont produces 2 million litres of maple syrup every year, the largest reserve of the sweet stuff in the USA. More than 150 farms, firms, and maple sugar houses produce the golden-brown syrup that Americans love to let drip over waffles and pancakes. In most of the enterprises visitors are heartily welcome: tours are even offered.

Lake Winnipesaukee   (106/C4)

New Hampshire's largest lake – the Indian name means "laughing water" and is of mythological origin – is part of a lowland plain full of lakes left behind by the Ice Age. The waters boast more than 200 islands, have a shoreline 290 km in length and are wreathed with villages from the 19th century. ❀ Lake Winnipesaukee can be explored with excursion boats *(MS "Mount Washington", 4 trips per day, from Weirs Beach, Tel. 603/366 55 31.* Guests may take the antique *Winnipesaukee Railroad*, which travels between Meredith and Laconia along the lake shore, transfer *(Tel. 603/279 52 53). Red Hill Inn (26 rooms; Route 25 B; Center Harbor; Tel. 603/279 70 01; Fax 279 70 03; category 2)* and the *Olde Orchard Inn (9 rooms; Lee Rd., Moultonborough; Tel. 603/476 50 04; Fax 476 54 19; category 2–3)* are old, attractively renovated overnight accommodations. Further addresses: *Greater Laconia Weirs Beach Chamber of Commerce; 11 Veterans Square, Laconia; Tel. 603/524 55 31 (Mon–Fri 9 am–5 pm)*

HANOVER

(106/B4) The city on the Upper Connecticut River is renowned for *Dartmouth College*, the northernmost of the so-called "ivy league" universities, to which well-heeled Americans traditionally send their youngsters. The noble progeny can be observed munching sandwiches in ⚑ *Old Pete's Tavern, 39 South Main St.* South of Hanover lies *Cornish*, a quiet, modest town with no less than four of those characteristically New England roofed bridges, among them Cornish-Windor Covered Bridge crossing the Connecticut River to Vermont, which, with a 138 m span is the longest. In and around Cornish artists such as the painter Maxfield Parrish and

Lake Winnipesaukee can be explored by boat

Whoever gets the votes wins the election

In one country with 50 states, competition is inevitable. An example: the presidential "primaries" are held every four years. According to history, the first of them took place in New Hampshire. A privilege jealously guarded as it guarantees a good turnover in hotels and restaurants and lots and lots of publicity. Since their neighbours in Vermont began to covet that number-one slot, by placing their own primary date earlier, New Hampshire simply enacted a law stating that New Hampshire votes on the Tuesday before the day on which any other New England state arranges a similar election.

the author J.D. Salinger (*The Catcher in the Rye*) have made their residence.

HOTELS

The Chase House
House from the 19th century on the Connecticut River. *8 rooms; Route 12 A, Cornish; Tel. 603/675 53 91; Fax 675 50 10; category 2*

The Hanover Inn
92 rooms on the campus of Dartmouth College. Pool, nice restaurant *Zins. The Green, Main St., Hanover; Tel 603/643 43 00; Fax 646 37 44; category 1*

INFORMATION

Hanover Chamber of Commerce
216 Main St.; Mon, Tues 9 am–2 pm, Wed–Sun 8 am–4.30 pm; Tel. 603/643 31 15

SURROUNDING AREA

Lake Sunapee **(106/C4)**
Lake Sunapee reminds one of the Alps (minus tourists and trucks!), ensconced among several state parks. Trips on steamers and cable railways departing from Sunapee yield give a fascinating view of the rugged, untouched landscape in the middle of New Hampshire. *Inn at Sunapee (Burkehaven Hill Rd.; Tel. 603/763 44 44; category 2–3)* is an old farmhouse with a venerable kitchen. Sport on Lake Sunapee: sailing and windsurfing.

KILLINGTON

(106/A4) The largest ski area east of the Rocky Mountains boasts over 18 ski slopes, the steepest ski-lifts and the wildest cat walk slope in the country. In the summer, golf and tennis top the list, alongside hiking and trout fishing. Music festivals enrich the cultural palette. From the summit of Mount Killington (1,260 m) one obtains a marvellous view over southern Vermont and the Green Mountain National Forest all the way to neighbouring Canada.

RESTAURANT

Hemingways
Creative American kitchen. *Dinner Wed–Sun; Route 4; Tel. 802/422 38 86; category 2*

The Vermont Inn
Farmhouse from the year 1840. Pool, tennis. *18 rooms; Route 4; Killington; Tel. 802/775 07 08; Fax 773 24 40; category 1–2*

Golf
Killington's Golf Course, snuggled between mountains and woods. *Killington Ski Area; Killington Rd.; Tel. 802/422 33 33*

Ski
The Killington ski area has 205 slopes. *Outer Limits* is said to be the most difficult. Lift tickets cost $54.60 per day *(Tel. 802/422 33 33)*. Through Killington there's a cross-county ski track, which transverses Vermont from south to north. *Information: Mountain Meadows; Tel. 802/775 70 77*

Killington and Pico Area Information
Route 4 E; Killington; Mon–Fri 9 am–5 pm; Tel. 802/773 41 81

New England Maple Museum   (106/B4)
History of the production and processing of maple syrup. *Route; Pittsford; Nov.–May daily 10 am–16 pm, otherwise 8.30 am–5.30 pm; admission $2.50; Tel. 802/483 94 14*

MANCHESTER N.H.

(**106/C5**) With its 100,000 inhabitants the largest city in New Hampshire and in the 19th century the textile centre of the US. It attracts workers from the friendly neighbour to the north, and they in turn have lent a Franco-Canadian flair to the area. Meanwhile, dominant on the Merrimack River are the electrical plants and paper/leather processing industries.

Currier Gallery of Art
Gallery with a collection of mouth-blown glass vases and photography from the 18th century *201 Myrtle Way; admission $5; Tel. 603/669 61 44*

MANCHESTER VT.

(**106/B5**) Since the 19th century a popular resort area on the west slope of the Green Mountains; among those enjoying increasing popularity as a ski area are *Bromley Mountain, Snow Valley* and *Stratton Mountain*. An ideal spot for taking in the view: ❧ the peak of *Big Equinox Mountain* (1,147 m), to whose summit only one road leads. Fishing is a tremendously popular sport in this region. In the *American Museum of Fly Fishing (Route 7 A; admission $7; Tel. 802/362 33 00)* the rods, reels and flies of famous fishermen such as Winslow Homer and General Patton are on display. Along the crossing of routes 7, 11 and 30 a collection of outlet stores has arisen.

Wildflowers
Vermont specialities in a charming inn called *Reluctant Panther. West Rd./Route 7 A; Tel. 802/362 25 68; category 2*

HOTEL

Manchester View Motel

36 rooms with terrace and
🔽 a wonderful view over
meadows. Pool, fishing, hiking
paths. *Route 7 A, Manchester; Tel.
802/362 27 39; Fax 362 21 99;
category 1–3*

SPORTS & LEISURE

Golf

The *Gleneagles*-golf course of
the elegant Equinox Hotel is
set on soft hilly terrain. *Route
7 A, Manchester Village; Tel.
802/362 32 23*

INFORMATION

Manchester and the Mountains Chamber of Commerce

*Adams Park Green, Mon–Fri 9 am–
5 pm, Sat 10 am–4 pm, Sun 9 am–
2 pm; Tel. 802/362 21 00*

SURROUNDING AREA

Green Mountain Flyer   (106/B5)

The *Green Mountain Flyer* oper-
ates with antique railway
coaches from the middle of June
to the beginning of Oct. Between *Bellows Falls* and *Chester*.
Magnificent in the autumn.
*Daily except Mon; Green Mountain
Railroad, Bellows Falls; Tel.
802/463 30 69*

Bike touring   (106/B5)

⭐ Cycle tours from inn to inn,
organised by *Cycle-Inn Vermont* in
Ludlow. Tel. 802/228 87 99

Vermont Country Store   (106/B5)

The Vermont Country Store in
Weston is an old-fashioned em-
porium packed with things the

country person needs. *Route
100; 15 km south of Ludlow; Tel.
802/824 31 84*

MONTPELIER

(106/B3) Vermont seat of government and the smallest capital of all
the 50 states (pop. 8,200). Worth
visiting: The *Vermont Museum (109
State St.; Tel. 802/828 22 91)* presents Vermont's history, which began with French settlers.

HOTEL

The Inn at Montpelier

Bed & Breakfast in a Colonial
style house in the centre of town.
*19 rooms; 147 Main St., Montpelier;
Tel. 802/223 27 27; Fax 223 07 22;
category 2*

SURROUNDING AREA

Floating Bridge   (106/B3)

The Floating Bridge of Brook-
field, a bridge, truly afloat, built in
1821 over Sunset Lake and still in
use today.

PORTSMOUTH

(107/D5) The city on the Atlantic,
at the mouth of the *Piscataqua
River*, reminds one that access to
the sea was a chief economic
factor in New Hampshire's development. Eight houses of
well-to-do businessmen and
ship owners, built in the 18th
and 19th centuries, can be visited along with personal effects
such as clothing and furnishings.
Newcomers to the area will find
the round tour somewhat sim-
plified by taking the marked
Portsmouth Trail. Proof that the
preservation of old building ma-

Portsmouth owes its importance to sea access

terials is worthwhile can be seen in Strawbery Banke on Marcy Street, where 35 houses have been restored and partially transformed into a spacious museum. There one can admire older tradesman's techniques. The *Portsmouth Trail* joins the most interesting points.

RESTAURANT

Oar House Restaurant
◉ New England specialities, good fish soups. *55 Ceres St.; Tel. 603/436 40 25; category 2*

HOTEL

Sise Inn
Queen-Anne style house from the year 1881 in the middle of the town centre. *34 rooms; 40 Court St., Portsmouth; Tel. and Fax 603/433 12 00; category 1–2*

INFORMATION

Greater Portsmouth Chamber of Commerce
500 Market St.; Mon–Fri 8.30 am–5 pm, Sat 10 am–5 pm, Sun 10 am–4 pm; Tel. 603/436 11 18

SURROUNDING AREA

Isles of Shoals   (107/D5)
Around the nine rocky Isles of Shoals are entwined the tales of pirates and sunken ships. Tours: *New Hampshire Seacoast Cruises; Rye Harbor State Marina; Route 1 A, Rye; Tel. 603/964 55 45, and Isles of Shoals Steamship Co.; 315 Market St., Portsmouth; Tel. 603/431 55 00*

ST. JOHNSBURY

(106/C2–3) The college town is the starting point for a trip to the Northeast Kingdom in the northeast of Vermont: a landscape of endless maple forests. Everything anyone ever wanted to learn about maple syrup, used to sweeten waffle and toast breakfasts across the land can be acquired at the *Original Maple Grove Museum & Factory (admission $1; Route 2, St Johnsbury; Tel. 802/748 51 41).*

HOTEL

Rabbit Hill Inn
Romantic cosiness and an innovative and inventive American

kitchen. *21 rooms; Route 18, Lower Waterford; Tel. 802/748 51 68; Fax 748 83 42; category 1 (inclusive half board)*

INFORMATION

Northeast Kingdom Chamber of Commerce

357 Western Ave., Mon–Fri 8.30 am–5 pm; Tel. 802/748 36 78, in the summer additional info stand on Main St.

STOWE

(106/B3) Winter sport spot and cool breezes in high summer at the foot of *Mount Mansfield*, which, with its 1,320 m, is the highest peak in Vermont (a Gondola leads to the top). North of Stowe, Route 108 leads through ☙ *Smuggler's Notch*, where rocky cliffs are so close together that they once offered smugglers their safe passage to Canada.

RESTAURANT

Season's Dining Room

At *Stowehof Inn* American dishes served in a Tirolean atmosphere. Breakfast and dinner. *Edson Hill Rd.; Tel. 802/253 97 22; category 2*

HOTEL

Trapp Family Lodge

The family hotel, rebuilt after a fire, does belong to that same Trapp family, who made famous by the filmmakers of Hollywood. Ski-cabin cosiness, tennis, pool. *93 rooms; Trapp Hill Rd., Stowe; Tel. 802/253 85 11; Fax 253 57 40; category 1–2*

SPORTS & LEISURE

Golf

The *Stowe Country Club* *(Tel. 802/253 48 93)* and the *Copley Country Club* *(Morrisville; Tel. 802/888 30 13)* are among the most beautiful places in the area.

Slide

The nearly 800-metre-long *Alpine Slide* on *Spruce Peak (Tel. 802/253 30 00)* is a favourite of children.

Ski

45 slopes, among them the especially difficult National, Liftline, Starr and Goat. A lift ticket costs $52. Cross-country fans find their trails in Stowe – 30 km of them.

INFORMATION

Stowe Area Association

Main St.; Tel. 802/253 73 21; Mon–Fri 9 am–8 pm, in summer also Sat, Sun 9 am–5 pm

WHITE MOUNTAINS

(106/C3) ★ ☙ *Mount Washington*, the majestic peak of the White Mountains, is, with 1917 m, the highest rise east of the Mississippi. One can reach the summit by road (one, incidentally, not without its hazards, $16 for auto and driver) via a 13-km-long serpentine, devoid of road dividers or guard rails. The peak can also be conquered by taking the first cog wheel railway, completed in 1869, to the top ($44). Or, of course, you can walk (free of charge). On the top arctic tundra awaits the visitor, a 100-km view of the *Presidential Range* and often stormy winds. A trip to the newly renovated *Mount Washington Hotel* in *Bretton Woods* illustrates that New Hampshire has for many generations been synonymous with summer holiday making. As many as 50 trains per day brought industrialists in private coaches at the beginning of the 20th century into the area where once the Indians presumed the Great Spirit to dwell. Bretton Woods became famous in 1944 as the meeting place of the International Monetary Fund (IWF), when here the system of stable exchange and the dollar as reserve currency was agreed upon.

The 50-km-long ❊ *Kancamagus Highway (Route 112)* between Lincoln and Conway is one of the most spectacular stretches for all those who wish to experience an *Indian Summer* in all its brilliance.

Franconia Notch offers a view of the dramatically formed ❊ incision in the world of mountains with the *Old Man of the Mountains,* a stone formation that looks like a head as its high point. In *North Conway,* the Mecca of the so-called *Outlet Stores,* one finds one business after another like pearls (or beads) on a string.

HOTEL

Franconia Inn
The guesthouse has been standing for some 150 years. Pool, tennis. Good restaurant. *35 rooms; Easton Rd./Route 116, Franconia; Tel. 603/823 55 42; Fax 823 80 78; category 1–2*

INFORMATION

Mount Washington Valley Chamber of Commerce
Main St., North Conway, Mon–Sat 9 am–5 pm; Tel. 603/356 31 71; Information at the train station: daily 10 am–8 pm.

Spectacular: a trip through the White Mountains

Beware: UFO abductions!

Lancaster, in the middle of the White Mountains of New Hampshire, may lay claim to being the scene of one of the most unbelievable occurrences in modern history: a human abduction by the crew of a UFO! Barney and Betty Hill were on their way from Canada to Portsmouth in September 1961, when they were followed and reportedly kidnapped by little green men, who all looked like the British-born comedian Bob Hope. The Hills lost consciousness and came to later in the vicinity of Concord. Their adventure was filmed in 1975.

WOODSTOCK

(106/B4) ★ Typical New England small town with covered bridge, green and well-maintained houses in the south of Vermont. The *Dana House (26 Elm St.; admission $1; Tel. 802/457 18 22)* offers valuable furniture from the 18th and 19th centuries. In the *Billings Farm and Museum (Route 12; admission $7; 2 km north of Woodstock; Tel. 802/457 23 55)* one can visit a historical farmhouse. The *Vermont Institute of Natural Science (Church Hill Rd.; Tel. 802/457 27 79)* displays owls, falcons and eagles from New England's north in its mini-zoo.

RESTAURANT

The Prince and the Pauper
French-influenced Vermont kitchen. One of the specialities of this restaurant: good home-made sausages. *24 Elm St.; Tel. 802/457 18 18; category 2*

HOTEL

The Woodstock Inn & Resort
You can find it at the green in the middle of Woodstock. Pool, golf, 10 tennis courts. *144 rooms; 14 The Green, Woodstock; Tel. 802/457 11 00; Fax 457 66 99; category 1*

INFORMATION

Woodstock Area Chamber of Commerce
18 Central St.; Mon–Fri 9.30 am–5.30 pm; Tel. 802/457 35 55; in summer information booth on the green; daily 8.30 am–5.30 pm; Tel. 802/457 10 42

SURROUNDING AREA

Quechee Gorge (106/B4)
Here the Ottauquechee River has formed a gorge 55 m deep. An impressive natural spectacle. Arrival via Route 4. There are several pleasant overnight accommodations in Quechee: *Quechee Inn at Marshland Farm* (with a charming country-elegant restaurant; *24 rooms; Clubhouse Rd.; Tel. 802/295 31 33; Fax 295 65 87; category 1*) and *Quechee Bed & Breakfast (8 rooms; Route 4; Tel. 802/295 17 76; no fax; category 2)*. The best place to eat is at the *Simon Pearce Restaurant (Main Street, Quechee; category 2)* in an old mill that was transformed into a glass-blowing factory.

The land of lighthouses and seclusion

A rugged sea coast, islands, mountains, clear rivers and lakes have lured summer holiday makers for generations

From a purely geographic standpoint, Maine, the northern corner of the US, accounts for one-half of New England. But this fact does overrate the value of the state to a certain degree. For the area along the Canadian border is a broad and lonely land with only 1.2 million inhabitants, 83 per cent covered by pine forests. The rocky coast, never monotonous, itself only 360 km in actual length, meanders over one thousand kilometres in and out of broken inlets, bays and river mouths. This landscape is, without a doubt, the major attraction of the largely unsettled state. Maine rates high on the list of preferred spots to spend the summer, and not only since President Bush established his summer residence in Kennebunkport.

It is the sea which has lent Maine it rugged face. And it is

Along the coast lighthouses guide the way

also the sea, in summer barely 16°C (61°F) warm, which delivers one of Maine's most famous products: ★ lobster.

Many of the old and delightful fishing villages from York on the border to New Hampshire to Cobscook Bay near the Canadian province New Brunswick offer this tasty delicacy. And though the price be sky high in other places, here the beloved crustaceans can also be had at more reasonable rates.

The coast is sectioned off into the divisions *South Coast* (from Piscataqua River to Portland), *Mid-coast* (up to Penobsot Bay) and *Downeast Coast*. The 2,000 forward positioned islands regardless of harsh wind and weather, present the most beautiful collection of lighthouses to be found in the US. The highpoint of every Maine trip: the strip of coast including *Acadia National Park* and its humped reddish mountains on *Mount Desert Island*.

The Acadia National Park has been a nature preserve since 1919

Inland, in the *Lakes and Mountains Region*, which reaches as far as New Hampshire and in *Aroostock County*, there's no scarcity of water. The 6,000 lakes and endless rivers are the playground of trout and those who wish to catch them. The surrounding pine woods belong to elks, lumberjacks and hunters.

Maine's cities are small by comparison. Portland, the largest, has only 61,000 inhabitants. It serves, much as does the capital Augusta, Bangor, Waterville or Presque Isle with schools, banks, businesses and state government offices, as administrative centre.

The French were – after the Vikings – the first Europeans in this part of America. They christened Maine after a region in their homeland, central France. For decades the territory was a bone of contention between the French and the English. Maine was finally, in 1677, purchased by the colony Massachusetts and in 1820 accepted into the Union as an independent state.

Maine enjoys its largest number of visitors in July and August, which is why it is advisable to seek assistance in finding accommodations from the *Maine Guide to Inns and B & B* (forwarded by the Maine Publicity Bureau).

ACADIA NATIONAL PARK

(105/E6) ★ The only National Park in the American northeast exists, since 1919, as a 150 sq km preserve for a splendid landscape of cliffs and crags. It extends over Mount Desert Island, the Schoodic Peninsula on the mainland and the small Isle au Haut. Mountains up to 460 m such as Mount Cadillac and steep rocks ledges rim the sleepy bays and provide a home to wild flowers, birds and mammals. A street, 45 km long, *Park Loop (begins 7 km north of Bar Harbor on Route 3)*, guarantees comfortable access. An exploration on foot, by horse-drawn carriage or bike is recommended. A fascinating alternative here: a trip on the Atlantic – comparatively tame in this area – by canoe or kayak. The best view of the National Park – visited yearly by some 3 million persons – is to be had from the peninsulas *Blue Hill* and *Hancock*.

RESTAURANT

Jordan Pond House
Rustic style with a view to *Jordan Pond*. Fish specialities. In the summer reservations are a must. *Park Loop Rd.; Tel. 207/276 33 16; category 2*

SPORTS & LEISURE

Cycles
Bar Harbor Bicycle Shop, 141 Cottage St., Bar Harbor; Tel. 207/288 38 86, and *Southwest Cycle, 370 Main St., Southwest Harbor; Tel. 207/244 58 56*

Kanu
Acadia Outfitters (106 Cottage St., Bar Harbor; Tel. 207/288 81 18) Here you have the possibility to rent kayaks and guides. The same offer: *National Park Canoe Rentals (Long Pond Inn; Tel. 207/244 58 54)*

Horse-drawn carriages
Wildwood Stables, Park Loop Rd.; Tel. 207/276 36 22

INFORMATION

Acadia National Park Visitors Centre
Hulls Cove; Tel. 207/288 33 38; May–Oct. daily 8 am–4.30 pm, in summer till 6 pm

SURROUNDING AREA

Isle au Haut **(105/D6)**
The little island is well suited for a one-day excursion on foot. There are hiking paths, isolated stretches of coast, an old midgets school and a general store waiting to be explored. *Boat from Stonington (Deer Isle); Tel. 207/367 51 93.* Romantic living: *The Keeper's House Inn* in the onetime lighthouse of the island *(Tel. 207/367 22 61; no fax; category 1 with three meals).*

MARCO POLO SELECTION: MAINE

1 **Acadia National Park**
Rose-coloured mountain swell and other natural wonders (page 76)

2 **Chebeague Island**
An insider tip at the end of the world (page 83)

3 **Freeport**
L. L. Bean shows how it's done: shopping in the middle of the night (page 81)

4 **Lobster**
Fresh from the Lobster Pound (page 75)

5 **Monhegan Island**
Rest and relaxation off the busy tourist path (page 79)

6 **Stonington on Deer Isle**
Old-time fishing village (page 80)

BAR HARBOR

(**105/E6**) The largest town, Mount Desert Island, gets its name from the French researcher Samuel de Champlain, the man who discovered the island with its bald peak in 1604. Due to its pleasant temperatures, in the latter years of the 19th century Bar Harbor became one of the holiday centres of rich American families such as the Rockefellers and Astors. Wooden mansions of every style, with up to 30 rooms, were not uncommon. In 1947 a fire destroyed many of these summer palaces. In the *Bar Harbor Historical Society (33 Ledgelawn Ave.;Tel. 207/288 00 00)* photos of the period of splendour can be viewed. Interesting as well: the ⬆ view from Cadillac Mountain.

RESTAURANTS

The Burning Tree
Run by a family of fishermen. *Route 3, Otter Creek; Tel. 207/ 288 93 31; category 2*

George's
Romantic. *7 Stephen's Lane; Tel. 207/288 45 05; category 2*

HOTELS

The Ledgelawn Inn
Former home of a wealthy Bostonian. *36 rooms; 66 Mount Desert St., Bar Harbor; Tel. 207/288 45 96; Fax 288 55 34; category 1*

Mira Monte Inn
13 rooms and 3 suites with balcony, fireplace and garden grounds. *69 Mount Desert St., Bar Harbor; Tel. 207/288 42 63; Fax 288 31 15; category 1–2*

INFORMATION

Bar Harbor Chamber of Commerce
93 Cottage St.; Tel. 207/288 51 03; in the summer Mon–Fri 8 am–6 pm

SURROUNDING AREA

Bass Harbor, Northeast Harbor, Seal Harbor and Southwest Harbor (**105/E6**)
Whoever entertains romantic thoughts concerning fishermen and lobster catchers will find both in the island towns of Seal Harbor, Northeast Harbor, Southwest Harbor and Bass Harbor. There, too, old "grand hotels" like the *Asticou Inn* in *Northeast Harbor (45 rooms; Route 3; Tel. 207/276 33 44; Fax 276 33 73; category 1)* have retained their glory. Kinder to the pocketbook is the *Bass Harbor Inn (Shore Rd.; Tel. 207/244 51 57; no fax; category 2–3).*

BOOTHBAY HARBOR

(**107/E3**) The former fishing village has become a pleasant refuge for tourists, no doubt because of the many boutiques, galleries and restaurants (the best ⬆ view to the harbour from *Andrew's Harborside, 8 Bridge St.).* Despite all the pretty decorations everything smells a lot like the sea and fish.

SIGHTS

Boothbay Railway Village
A reconstructed New England village at the turn of the century including a museum and 50 old-

timer autos. *Route 27; 2 km north of Boothbay; mid-June–mid-Oct.; admission $7; Tel. 207/633 47 27*

The Howard House
Noble motel class. Peaceful. *14 rooms; Townsend Ave./Route 27, Booth Bay Harbor; Tel. 207/633 39 33; Fax 633 62 44; category 3*

SPORTS & LEISURE

The piers are the starting point for boat trips and sailing tours to the small islands along the coast. *Captain Bob Fish (Pier 1; Tel. 207/633 26 26)* offers seal and whale watching tours as well as a lighthouse tour. Also worth a trip: *Clambake Cruises* to *Cabbage Island (Pier 6; Tel. 207/633 72 00).*

INFORMATION

Boothbay Harbor Region Chamber of Commerce
Route 27; Mon–Fri 9 am–5 pm; Tel. 207/633 23 53; in summer daily 9 am until 5 pm; Information at the intersection Route 1/Route 27

SURROUNDING AREA

Monhegan Island   (107/F3)
★ From Boothbay Harbor a ferry sets out to *Monhegan Island (Pier 8; Tel. 207/633 22 84)*. Portuguese and Briton fishermen once sailed along the steep cliffs of the island before Columbus reached America. The *Monhegan Museum* in the lighthouse gives an overview of the island's history. The *Island Inn (34 rooms; Tel. 207/596 03 71; Fax 594 55 17; category 1–2)* offers a good view

of the harbour and a romantic background for an overnight stay on a tidy little island with no autos. *Other opportunities: to set over from Port Clyde*

CAMDEN

(**107/F2**) Here up the up to 400-m-high foothills of the Camden Chain meet the Atlantic. The area is starting point for exploring the harbours and islands in Penobscot Bay as well as for an-

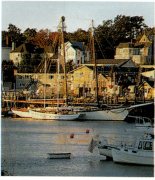

Lost in a dream: harbour of Camden

chor drop fishing boats and excursion windjammers. Shops and restaurants are found on Main St. and Bayview St.

RESTAURANT

Whitehall Inn
Imaginative fish specialities. *52 High St./Route 1; dinner mid-June–mid-Oct.; Tel. 207/236 33 91; category 2*

HOTEL

Camden Harbor Inn
Formerly the accommodation of ship passengers. Star-restau-

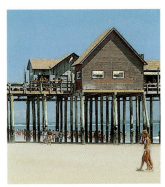

Pole constructions have a long tradition on the shores in New England

rant with fish specialities. *22 rooms; 83 Bayview St., Camden; Tel. 207/236 42 00; Fax 236 70 63; category 1*

SPORTS & LEISURE

Sailing cruises
The schooner "Mary Day" sails with up to 30 passengers three, four or six day tours along the coast. *P.O. Box 798, Camden; Tel. 207/785 56 70*

INFORMATION

Rockport-Camden-Lincolnville Chamber of Commerce
Commercial St./Public Landing, Camden; Tel. 207/236 44 04; Mon–Fri 9 am–5 pm, in summer also Sat 10 am–5 pm and Sun 12 am–4 pm

SURROUNDING AREA

Islesboro Island (107/F2)
On the island Islesboro rich families in search of seclusion, have for generations constructed expansive summer houses. The island can be best explored by bike (to rent: *Maine Sport; Route 1; 3 km south of Camden; Tel. 207/236 87 97).* Ferry: *Maine State Ferry Service; Lincolnville Beach; Tel. 207/789 56 11*

Rockland (107/F3)
In the *Farnsworth Art Museum* are found paintings of a Maine artist family: N.C., Andrew and Jamie Wyeth. *356 Main St.; admission $8; Tel. 207/596 64 57*

Tenants Harbor (107/F3)
Route 131 leads to a typical Maine harbour still characterized more by lobstermen than T-shirt shops: Tenants Harbor.

DEER ISLE

(105/D6) The island, located directly before the mainland, can only be reached by a bridge. It is surrounded on the Penobscot Bay and Blue Hill Bay sides by hundreds of tiny, pine-covered islands. Particularly beautiful is the view from *Caterpillar Hill (2 km south of the junction Route 15 and Route 175).* ★ Stonington is still a harbour for many fishing boats, but Main St. has already changed into a busy shopping strip.

RESTAURANT

Fisherman's Friend
◉ Simple fish restaurant, good and reasonable. No credit cards. *School St., Stonington; Tel. 207/367 24 42; category 3*

HOTEL

Pilgrim's Inn
A 200-year-old inn. Cosy restaurant – reservations a must!

15 rooms; Deer Isle; Tel. 207/ 348 66 15; Fax 348 77 69; category 1

Deer Isle-Stonington Chamber of Commerce
Route 15; Little Deer Isle; Mon–Fri 9 am–4 pm; Tel. 207/348 61 24

FREEPORT

(107/E3) ★ The shopping capital of Maine, famous throughout America since the mail-order house *L.L. Bean* opened a shop in which offers patrons casual clothing, hunting, hiking and fishing outfits and all that goes with them *(Main St./Route 1; Tel. 207/865 47 61)* round the clock. Meanwhile some 100 additional shops have opened their doors on Main St. and Bow St.

HOTEL

The Harraseeket Inn
Former farmhouse whose 84 rooms are furnished with antiques. First-class restaurant and bar. *162 Main St., Freeport; Tel. 207/865 93 77; Fax 865 16 84; category 1*

KENNEBUNKPORT

(107/E4) Traditional bathing spot and holiday residence of ex-President George Bush *(House at Walker's Point). Dock Square* is the centre of this busy little summer town with galleries and shops. *Captains' houses* from the 19th century and the residences of wealthy summer guests beautify Maine, Pearl and Green St. In the *Seashore Trolley Museum (Log Cabin*

Rd.; Tel. 207/967 27 12) the largest collection of trolley wagons in the world is to be found.

RESTAURANT

Mabel's Lobster Claw
◆ Mabel's lobster stuffed with Jakob's oysters have the reputation of being ex-President George Bush's favourite dish. *124 Ocean Ave.; Tel. 207/967 25 62; category 2*

HOTELS

Captain Jefferds Inn
Captain's house from 1804. *15 rooms; Pearl St., Kennebunkport; Tel. 207/967 23 11; Fax 967 07 21; category 1–2*

The Ocean View
With ❧ a sea view. *9 rooms; 171 Beach Ave., Kennebunk Beach; Tel. 207/967 27 50; Fax 967 54 18; category 1–2*

INFORMATION

Kennebunk-Kennebunkport Chamber of Commerce
17 Western Ave.; Mon–Fri 9 am– 5 pm, in summer also Sat, Sun 10 am–2 pm; Tel 207/967 08 57

MOOSEHEAD LAKE

(104/C4) On the southern shore of the largest lake in Maine with a shoreline of 600 km and a form resembling the head of a moose, lies *Greenville* – starting point for numerous sports activities: raft and dinghy trips on *Moosehead Lake*, on the *Penobscot* and the *Allagash River*, fishing (salmon, trout) from May to Sept., pheasant, bear and moose hunting in Nov. and Dec. *Experienced guides can be booked via sports shops.*

HOTEL

Greenville Inn
Former residence of a lumber baron, with a sea view. You can find an austrian inspired restaurant. *9 rooms; Norris St., Greenville; Tel. 207/695 22 06; Fax 695 03 35; category 1–2*

SPORTS & LEISURE

Fishing
Maine Guide Fly Shop, Main St.; Tel. 207/695 22 66

Kanu
Allagash Canoe Trips; Pleasant St.; Tel. 207/695 36 68

INFORMATION

Moosehead Lake Region Chamber of Commerce
Route 15; Greenville; daily 9 am– 5 pm, in winter Mon–Fri 10 am–4 pm; Tel. 207/695 27 02

SURROUNDING AREA

Baxter State Park (104–105/C–D3)
The nature preserve is home to the 1,600-metre-high *Mount Katahdin*, Maine's highest mountain and the beginning of a 3,477-km-long trek, known as the the *Appalachian Trail* (it ends in Georgia). The Native Americans referred to the elevation as "God with Head in the Clouds". The original landscape looks, as the American author Henri Thoreau put it, as if it had rained huge rocks. *Tel. 207/723 51 40*

OGUNQUIT

(107/D4) Known once among the Indians as "beautiful place at the water", the town has been a sea spa and artist colony since the 1880s. The *Museum of Art* lies close to the beach *(Shore Rd.; Tel. 207/646 49 09)* and has a sculpture garden with a view to the sea. *Bald Head Cliff* offers a view to the coast, particularly romantic when the weather turns stormy. Good lobster in the *Ogunquit Lobster Pond* and at *Arrows.*

HOTEL

The Terrace by the Sea
Noble motel style. View to the sea. *36 rooms; 11 Wharf Lane, Ogunquit, ME 03907; Tel. 207/ 646 32 32; no fax; category 2*

SPORTS & LEISURE

Lobster fishing
While at sea a lobsterman demonstrates how the tasty crustaceans are nabbed. *Finestkind Cruises, Perkins Cove; Tel. 207/ 646 52 27*

INFORMATION

Ogunquit Information Center
Route 1; in summer daily 9 am– 5 pm; Tel. 207/646 55 33

PORTLAND

(107/E4) The harbour town has developed into the cultural and economic centre of the state, though it was once almost completely destroyed by the Indians in the 17th century, by English cannons in the 18th and by a raging fire in the 19th. Portland, which lies almost 200 km closer to Europe than any other American harbour for seagoing vessels, is only just entering the modern period. Warehouses and office buildings on the port have been transformed into businesses and restaurants.

MUSEUM

Portland Museum of Art

American masterpieces by Winslow Homer to Andrew Wyeth in a modern building by the famous architect I. M. Pei. *7 Congress Square; Mon, Tues, Thurs, Sat, Sun 10 am–5 pm; Wed, Fri 10 am–9 pm; admission $6; Tel. 207/775 61 48*

HOTEL

Portland Regency Inn

Right in the middle of the Old Port Exchange. *95 rooms; 20 Milk St., Portland; Tel. 207/774 42 00; Fax 775 21 50; category 1*

SPORTS & LEISURE

Ferries and excursion boats set out from the Portland and State piers. The ◁▷ *Casco Bay Lines (Tel. 207/774 78 71)* travel to the 140 Calendar Islands, among them *Peaks Island. Eagle Island*, residence of the North Pole explorer Robert E. Peary, is the destination of a 4-hour tour by *"Kristy K."* (Long Wharf; Tel. 207/774 64 98).

INFORMATION

Visitors Information Center

305 Commercial St.; Tel. 207/772 58 00; Mon–Sat 8 am–6 pm, Sun 10 am–6 pm (in summer), Mon–Fri 8 am–5 pm, Sat, Sun 10 am–3 pm (in winter)

SURROUNDING AREA

Chebeague Island (107/E3)

★ ◁▷ One hour from the mainland (via *Casco Bay Lines, Commercial St.*). The 8-km-long, wildly romantic island has both sand and rock beaches, a *9-hole golf course* and the ◆ *Chebeague-Island Inn*, where the island's inhabitants meet in the evening for a beer *(21 rooms; Box 492, Chebeague Island; Tel. 207/846 51 55; Fax 846 42 65).*

YORK

(107/D5) The network of streets dating from the 18th and 19th centuries, alone make a visit to York Village worthwhile. Visit the old *Lighthouse* of Cape Neddick at the end of York Beach!

SIGHTS

York Historical Society

A prison from the year 1720 along with six homes have been combined to make a museum. *Tickets in Gaffard's Tavern; Lindsay Rd.; mid-June–mid-Sept.; Tues–Sat 10 am–4 pm; admission $7; Tel. 207/363 49 74*

HOTEL

Dockside Guest Quarters

On an island in York Harbor. *25 rooms; Harris Island Rd., York; Tel. 207/363 28 68; Fax 363 19 77; category 1–3*

INFORMATION

The Yorks Chamber of Commerce

Route 1, York; Tel. 207/363 44 22; in summer daily 9 am–5 pm, in winter Mon–Fri 10 am–4 pm

Playground for New York's society

*Long Island: empty beaches, soft breakers
and a breath of exclusivity*

Even if it does belong to the State of New York politically and geographically it does not quite fit into New England – "Long Island", pointing northwards from Manhattan like some elongated finger has much in common with its mainland neighbours in New England. It begins with a shared history of fishing and whaling and extends to a sense of tradition of cosy small-town tidiness on to a related architecture and a considerable cultural palette. Long Island's major attraction is its long and empty beaches and soft Atlantic surf.

The flair of well-to-do residents with splendid wooden houses, well-tended gardens and exclusive clubs for polo, hurdle springing and golf is especially noticeable starting at the end of the south side, at South Fork between Westhampton and Montauk. Since 1870, when the Long Island Railroad linked the island to

This is where the New Yorkers meet on the weekends: Southampton

New York as a near-by recreation area, the fascination with the flatter-than-flat landscape with its former potato fields as well as its fresh sea breezes in the middle of a hot and sultry summer all remain unabated. Long Island is a welcome change from the noise and hustle of the city.

The beaches are, as everywhere in America, public drivers must, however, pay a high parking fee. That is also one reason why the bicycle has established itself as the ideal means of transportation on Long Island. The other reason: travelling at bike tempo allows one to see much more of the old houses and meticulously tended gardens.

Well-heeled New Yorkers erected the first wooden palaces, with their grey shingles, white columns, arches and towers on the then still virgin dunescape at the end of the 19th century. Upon immaculate lawns one played croquette, drank iced tea and enjoyed, sitting back on wicker chairs from one's veranda, the cool breeze of the Atlantic.

Meanwhile the old villas have new neighbours. Many built without any recognisable style. One finds small *Saltbox*-wooden houses, true to the tradition, nestled beside gargantuan neo-classical mansions with colonnades alongside the artistry of innovative architects.

Incidentally: when New Yorkers speak of Long Island, they mean the Hamptons. Also meaning a very specific social stratum: an unconventional mixture of money and taste, glamour and understatement, that reminds one of European sea spas and summer holidays away. News as well as trends are found in the *East Hampton Star*, in *Dan's Paper*, in *Hampton's Magazine* and the magazine *Hampton Country*.

The season kicks off traditionally on Memorial Day (the last Monday in May) and lasts until Labor Day (first Monday in September). During this period the main traffic arteries (Long Island Expressway = I-495 and Route 27, named Sunrise Highway) are packed, the overnight prices for accomodation are 40 per cent higher than normal and most hotels demand a minimum stay of two if not three days.

★ The best advice is to book a stay after the Great Attack, when everything smells of baking potatoes and autumn is in the air, with the local residents once again among their own. (Nights are then relatively cool!)

Leaving New York you reach the Hamptons by bus: *Hampton Jitney; reservation under Tel. 800/936 04 40 or 516/283 46 00. Departure from 40th St. between Lexington and Third Ave., at 59th or 69th St. the corner of Lexington Ave. or from 86th St. between 3rd and Lexington Ave. ($22)*. The best mode of transportation once there: a bicycle.

BRIDGEHAMPTON

(**108/C5**) On the main drag one strolls from one antique shop to another. The favourite meeting place of the old-timers of Long Island is the *Sagpond General Store* – especially mornings, when one picks up one's obligatory copy of the *New York Times*. They're always there, a paper cup of coffee in hand. Not to be missed: a visit to *Sagpond Vineyards (139 Sagg Rd.; Tel. 516/537 51 06)*, where the landlord Christian Wölffer and his wine steward Roman Roth produce Chardonnays and Merlots. Wine tasting is free of charge.

RESTAURANTS

Alison By The Beach
Outlet of one of the elegant Manhattan bistros with French kitchen and a particularly good Bouillabaisse. *Montauk Highway (Townline St.); Tel. 516/537 71 00; category 1–2*

The Candy Kitchen
Hampton family diner. Excellent hamburgers. *Montauk Highway; Tel 516/537 98 85; category 3*

95 School Street
In following both the trend of organic farming and genetic production, the biologically-dynamic ingredients come from breeders and farmers from the area. The lobster with basil sauce is outstanding. *School St.; Tel 516/537 55 55; category 1–2*

MARCO POLO SELECTION: LONG ISLAND

1 Autumn on Long Island
Fog and the scent of baked potatoes (page 86)

2 Lobster or tuna fish steak
Best at Gosman's on the dock at Montauk Harbor (page 89)

3 Main Beach of East Hampton
From here one can run all the way to Montauk (page 87)

4 Main Street in Southampton
Seeing and being seen (page 92)

ENTERTAINMENT

Wild Rose Cafe
Popular spot for blues music with lively bar. *Sag Harbor Turnpike; Tel 516/537 50 50*

EAST HAMPTON

(108–109/C–D5) Around the immaculately tended green are the patriarchal houses of rich New York scions with a family tree extending back to the 17th century. Main St. and Newton Lane are dotted with antique shops, noble boutiques (among them, Ralph Lauren and Donna Karan) and restaurants. Several prominent residents of East Hampton line on the contemplative, Further Lane, among others, the singer Billy Joel. ★ *Main Beach* is numbered among the especially beautiful stretches on the east coast.

Neighbouring *Amagansett* also ranks high on the house owners' and summer guests' list. One "belongs" when one buys at *Amagansett Farmer's Market* – and nowhere do coffee and croissants taste better than on the wooden tables in front of the market, from which one can comfortably observe the goings-on.

RESTAURANTS

Della Famina
Considered the favourite meeting place of prominence. On the menu you find goose liver from the Hudson Valley and halibut from Maine. *99 North Main St.; Tel 516/329 66 66; category 1–2*

East Hampton Point
Lunch or drinks on the terrace at Three Mile Harbor. *Three Mile Harbor Rd.; Tel. 516/329 28 00; category 1–2*

Nick & Tony's
An Italian restaurant with many famous customers. *136 N Main St.; Tel. 516/324 35 50; category 1–2*

Pacific East
Innovative fish dishes. *415 Main St., Amagansett; Tel. 516/267 77 70; category 2*

Peconic Coast
A chef arrived from Paris to lend the menu of this lively lounge the flair of southern France. *103 Montauk Highway; Tel 516/324 67 72; category 2*

Amagansett House
An old farm house as pleasant B & B. *4 rooms; Main St., Amagansett; Tel. 516/267 38 08; category 1–2*

The Maidstone Arms
Oldest inn in the area dating from the 18th century with an attractive restaurant and garden. *19 rooms; 207 Main St., East Hampton; Tel. 516/324 50 06; Fax 324 50 37; category 1*

Sea Breeze Inn
Nice little house hear the beach. *12 rooms; 30 Atlantic Ave., Amagansett; Tel. 516/267 36 92; Fax 267 86 21; category 2*

The Hedges Inn
Directly on the green in the centre of town and thus convenient for shopping and beach. *11 rooms; 74 James Lane, East Hampton; Tel. 516/324 71 00; Fax 324 58 16; category 1*

Bicycles
Bermuda Bikes, 36 Gingerbread Lane; Tel. 516/324 66 88; Village Hardware, 32 Newton Lane; Tel. 516/324 24 56

Stephen's Talk House
Live music with well-known old stars. *Main St., Amagansett; Tel. 516/267 31 17*

East Hampton Chamber of Commerce
79-A Main St.; Mon–Fri 10 am–4 pm, Sat 11 am–4 pm, in winter Tues–Sat

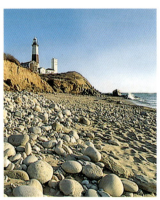

One flees New York and seeks peace on near-by Long Island

The Hamptons: stars without airs

A house on Long Island, direct on the beach between Westhampton and East Hampton, is a status symbol in America. "Cashhamptons" is how these areas are referred to, because here money, power and fame merge. This is all tastefully fringed by a number of prominent persons from the fields of art and literature. Musicians like Paul Simon, film makers like Steven Spielberg, fashion designers like Calvin Klein, writers like Kurt Vonnegut and Tom Wolfe (who also makes his way to the beach clad in an immaculate white suit) are only a few of the luminaries who make Long Island their home. One can do some "star spotting" during the summer in pubs, while biking or shopping. Here apparently they feel at home – stars devoid airs.

Playground for New York's high society: the Hamptons

10 am–4 pm; Tel. 516/324 03 62.
Offers on the Internet under
www.peconic.net – a complete listing
of all accommodations in the eastern
end of Long Island.

MONTAUK

(**109/D5**) In the shadow of the light-house on the east end of Long Island, built in 1797 at the request of George Washington, one has the feeling of having arrived at the ends of the earth. The area is a mixture of marshland and dunes, where back in 1926 an investor wished to build the "Miami Beach of the North". The Great Depression at the end of the 1920s put an end to the project. Only in the 1970s did they begin building again – private apartments and motels. Despite these transgressions Montauk has not lost the flair of an old fishing village. One notices it especially when the morning boats sail in.

Numerous "clam bars" line the Montauk Highway (Route 27). One is the *The Lobster Roll*, named for the fabulous bread rolls with fresh lobster salad they offer for picnics on the beach *(close to Napeague Beach).*

Gosman's
★ Direct on the pier, where the fishing boats land. Lobster from $16.95. *Gosman's Dock, Flamingo Rd.; Tel. 516/668 53 30; category 2*

Lenhart Cottages
12 cottages, view to the dunes or sea. *Old Montauk Highway; Tel. and Fax 516/668 23 56; category 1–2*

Montauk Yacht Club
Noble accommodations with private boat harbour, pools, tennis

courts and restaurants. *107 rooms; Star Island; Tel. 516/668 31 00; Fax 668 61 86; category 1*

Panoramic View

Located directly on the beach. The prettiest rooms you can find in the Salt Sea House. *118 rooms; 272 Old Montauk Highway; Tel. 516/668 30 00; Fax 668 78 70; category 1–2*

Peri's

B & B with 3 rooms; also offers massage and cosmetic treatment. *206 Essex St.; Tel. 516/668 13 94; Fax 668 60 96; category 1*

SPORTS & LEISURE

Boattrips

Whale watching trips arranged by the Ocean Research Founda-

tion. *Departure: Viking Dock; Tel. 516/369 98 40*

Bicycle

Montauk Bike Shop, Main St.; Tel. 516/668 89 75

Golf

Montauk Downs, an 18-hole course open to all and sundry remains one of the ten most outstanding golf courses in the US. *S Fairview Ave.; Tel. 516/668 50 00 (Green fee: $30/35)*

INFORMATION

Montauk Chamber of Commerce

Helps with finding accommodation. *The Plaza; Tel 516/668 24 28; Mon–Fri 10 am–4 pm, in summer Mon–Fri 10 am–5 pm, Sat 10 am–4 pm, Sun 10 am–2 pm*

Weather-worn frame houses dot the shore along Long Island

NORTH FORK

(**108/C5**) On the northern arm of the Long Island tongue, time seems to have stood still: the farmers have not yet sold their land to property-hungry speculators from New York. There are still many small farms and as of recently also a number of vineyards (e. g. *Paumanok* in *Jamesport* or *Bedell Cellars* and *Pellegrini* in *Cutchogue)*. One purchases fresh produce at *farm stands* (i.e., in *Mattituck, East Marion* and *Orient)*, the catch of the day directly at the water *(The Seafood Barge, Main Rd., Southold; Tel. 516/765 30 10; or Orient by the Sea, Main Rd.; Orient Point; Tel. 516/323 24 24)*. From *Orient Point* one catches the auto ferry to Shelter Island and reaches South Fork, business a spin-off of Hampton.

HOTELS

Motel on the Bay
19 simple rooms to be found on Peconic Bay with its own private beach. *Front St. S, Jamesport; Tel. 516/722 34 58; Fax 722 51 66; category 1–2*

Townsend Manor Inn
The onetime house of a whaling captain is situated at the harbour of Jamesport. Pool. *23 rooms; 714 Main St., Jamesport; Tel. 516/477 20 00; Fax 477 25 03; category 2*

INFORMATION

North Fork Chamber of Commerce
In summer Mon–Fri 9 am– 5 pm; Main Rd., Greenport; Tel. 516/477 13 83

SAG HARBOR

(**108/C5**) The former whaling port on the north side of Long Island is proud to guarantee a contrasting summer program to the celebrity side-show in Westhampton, Southampton and East Hampton. The slogan goes: "The Hamptons minus Hampton Follies".

The relative serenity has lured artists and writers for generations. The *Whaling Museum (Main St.;Tel. 516/692 96 26)* tells the stories of the whalers and their ships. Main St., full of character and brimming with tradition, is adorned with tasteful boutiques and an entire series of good restaurants.

RESTAURANT

The Beacon
French cuisine and terrace with ⬇ harbour view. *8 W Water St.; Tel. 516/725 70 88; category 2–3*

HOTELS

American Hotel
Victorian decor in a brick building which is protected as a historical site. *8 rooms; Main St.; Tel. 516/ 725 35 35;Fax 725 35 73;category 1*

The Inn at Baron's Cove
66 rooms (from $155) with ⬇ a view to the small harbour and the possibility to cook one's own meals. Tennis. Pool. *31 W.Water St.; Tel. 516/725 21 00; Fax 725 21 44; category 1*

INFORMATION

Sag Harbor Chamber of Commerce
Main St.; June–Oct. Mon–Fri 10 am–2 pm; Tel. 516/725 00 11

SHELTER ISLAND

(108/C5) A large part of the island in Gardiner's Bay, between the fork prongs of Long Island, was, in former times, the hide-away for pirates, persecuted Quakers, bathtub gin makers and well-heeled big-city boys. Another way of describing the <mark>nature preserve</mark> *Mashomack* is a nesting spot for sea eagles. *Ferry connection from North Haven (South Fork) and Greenport (North Fork).*

HOTELS

Chequit Inn
Old summer sea-hotel with stylish veranda. Good restaurant. *35 rooms; Shelter Island Heights; Tel. 516/749 00 18; Fax 749 01 83; category 1–3*

Ram's Head Inn
Stately shingle villa with a view over Coecles Harbor. Outstanding restaurant with French-influenced cuisine. *17 rooms; Shelter Island Heights; Tel. 516/749 08 11; Fax 749 00 59; category 1–2*

SOUTHAMPTON

(108/C5) The *Historic Walking Trail* leads from *Southampton Historical Museum (Meeting House Lane (Tel. 516/283 24 94))* to the historical kernel of the largest town at the end of Long Island (pop. 4,000). In a triangle formed of ★ Main Street, Job's Lane and Hampton Road you'll find the most beautiful small shops on the entire island: the place to be seen on weekends. Also a very popular place to meet: *Cooper's Beach* and *Town Beach.*

MUSEUM

Parrish Art Museum
American artists. *25 Job's Lane; Mon–Sat 11 am–5 pm, Sun 1 pm–5 pm; admission $2; Tel. 516/283 21 18*

RESTAURANTS

Basilico
Noble trattoria with Tuscany ambiance. *10 Windmill Lane; Tel. 516/283 79 87; category 2*

Lobster Inn
The speciality of the house is lobster, lobster and then a bit more lobster. *162 Inlet Rd.; Tel. 516/283 15 25; category 2*

75 Main
US cuisine, inspired by the Far East. Spring rolls of duck meat and lamb with Thai-spices. *75 Main St.; Tel. 516/283 02 02; category 2*

HOTEL

B & B Reservation Service of Southampton
Besides the 8 rooms at home, private rooms are also arranged between $100 and $400. *579 Hill St.; Tel. 516/287 09 02; Fax 287 62 40; category 1–2*

SPORTS & LEISURE

Beach
★ Cooper's Beach *(parking fee: $15, on the weekend: $20)*

INFORMATION

Southampton Chamber of Commerce
76 Main St.; Mon–Fri 10 am–4 pm, Sat, Sun 11 am–3 pm; Tel. 516/283 04 02

Nature and Culture for Connoisseurs

The routes are marked in green on the map on the inside front cover and in the Road Atlas beginning on page 104

in the Road Atlas beginning on page 104

① WIND, SAND, SEA: WHERE BOSTONIANS TAKE HOLIDAYS

 Starting from on the tracks of the Kennedys to Cape Cod and Nantucket. Time: depending on your place about 3–5 days.

Summer holidays mean to *Bostonians (p. 40)*: finding small, secluded spots with sea spa flair, ones that even at the height of the tourist season are not over-run with tourists. And why? Aside from a series of Bed & Breakfasts found on Cape Cod, Nantucket and Martha's Vineyard there is no hotel tourism worth mentioning. Whoever takes his holidays there either owns a house or is lucky enough to rent one.

The first visitors to *Cape Cod (p. 46)*, which resembles a flexed arm with clenched fist, were the Pilgrim Fathers from Britain, whose descendants lived chiefly from fishing. Later came painters who founded an artists' colony. All together they succeeded in creating the atmosphere that envelops one the mo-

ment one travels Route 6 A over the *Sagamore Bridge* via the Cape Cod Canal which was completed in 1914 to reach *Sandwich (p. 48)*, the oldest settlement on the Cape. The village abides with its typically white frame houses, duck ponds and a mill. Buildings like the *Hoxie House* go back to the second half of the 17th century. Through the marshlands it goes on to *Barnstable*, where the street is seamed with junk shops, galleries and Bed & Breakfasts. Continuing on to the north, the roads lead to the beaches of Cape Cod Bay, the most stunning of which, *Sandy Neck Beach*, extends over 10 km of dunes. The trip in an easterly direction through a patch which the locals call *Mid Cape*, leads through *Yarmouth* and *Brewster*, where the splendid houses built by the seafaring captains still proudly stand. In *Orleans* the route takes a sharp turn to the north and runs from that point along Route 6. You pass by an extraordinarily beautiful landscape: *Cape Cod National Seashore*, an area that was placed under protection as a nature preserve in 1961. The stretch is nearly 50 km in length: immaculate, white sand behind the dunes, marshes and low woods – in its perfection it seems more a painting than reality. Visit the *Salt Pond Visitor Center* in *Eastham*, where you have access to the beach as well as to a great deal of useful information. On the way to the tip of the Cape, you come to the *Lower Cape* first through *Wellfleet*, a quiet spot that seems almost to doze off in the time between September and June. It is famous for its oysters, its galleries and for having the largest flea market on the peninsula. The contrast to *Provincetown (p. 48)*, at the end of the Cape, set in its "fist", could hardly be greater. "P-Town" and its overwhelmingly gay summer guests make the areas around Commercial Street lively but loud.

While there is only one country road for the way back to the narrow *Lower Cape* (Route 6), you can find alternatives for the *Mid Cape*. For instance Route 28, which forks off in Orleans in the direction of *Chatham*. From there you reach, via Main Street, *Hyannis* and, just off the coast, *Hyannisport (p. 47)*, the summer retreat of the Kennedy dynasty. A permanent exhibition in the *John F. Kennedy Hyannis Museum* on Main Street pays tribute to the special relationship of the family from Boston to Cape Cod. Hyannis is the place where you should leave your auto parked to take the ferry for an excursion to the one-time whalers' island *Nantucket (p. 54)*. The picture-book town with its cliffs and houses sided with grey wooden shingles can best be explored by bike. Also: in summertime all auto space on the ferry is rented out months in advance. Back to Cape Cod, now to *Falmouth (p. 47)* where the green is fringed by houses from the 19th century. Last station on the way back is Sagamore Bridge once again.

② HIGH SPIRITS IN THE NORTH: MOUNTAINOUS AND COLOURFUL

 Departing from Concord into the colourful display presented by the woods of Vermont and New Hampshire, on to Mount Washington and the oldest villages of the Colonial Period. Time: about 7 days.

The striking face of original New England with its impassable mountains, endless woods and uncounted lakes are to be found inland – in New Hampshire and Vermont. A number of prominent American writers have also found their way here in search of solitude. While the white frame houses create the impression that time has stood still, the brief crescendo of the multicoloured maple and oak forest soon teaches one the error of one's ways. As short and illusine as *Indian Summer* may be – it returns each year. A trip to the mountainous country of New England should be undertaken from Boston via I 93 and begin in *Concord (p. 65, Exit 13)*. In the capital of New Hampshire, the lawmakers of the state have met under the gilded dome of the capitol since 1819. The charm lies in the contrast to the village scenes one can discover if one decides to depart the town via the I 393. Travelling eastwards, turn after a few kilometres on to Route 106 and continue north. This is the road to *Canterbury Village*, one of the few relics from the time when the religious community of Shakers was resident here. A simple glance conveys the impressive simplicity of the group's style of living, whose last member died in 1992.

Travelling north you follow Route 106, then Route 3, to reach *Lake Winnipesaukee (p. 66)*. It is a portion of a vast plain of lakes left behind by the Ice Age. The lake with a more than 250 km shoreline can be best explored by excursion boat from *Weirs Beach* on the northwest shore. Further to the north *(turn off in Meredith)* take Route 25 and then Route 16 *(turn off in West Ossipee)* to the next destination – the shopping mile of *North Conway*. The place has numerous "outlet stores" of brand-name consumer article manufacturers. It is also the starting point for a drive up to *Mount Washington (p. 71)*, the highest elevation (1,917 m) east of the Mississippi, from whose wind-blown peak one can see a good 100 km when the weather is good – all the way to the steep swells of the White Mountains, which characterize New Hampshire's north. Go back over the same serpentine down to the valley on to Route 16 to the south fork of Route 302 in *Glen*. This is the stretch to *Bretton Woods (p. 71)*, where the imposing Mount Washington Hotel stands, in which in 1944 two significant institutions were founded – the International Monetary Fund and the World

Bank. Further to the west the street meets Route 3, with which, travelling south, you drive through *Franconia Notch State Park*. Its highpoints are the naturally formed, wild-appearing granite creations *Old Man of the Mountain* and *The Flume*, a deep incision in the rocky face of the landscape. Following Route 112 *(turn off in North Woodstock)* and continuing westwards cut through the last section of the picturesque *White Mountains (p. 71)*.

At the intersection with Route 302 the road goes down to the left into the *Valley of the Connecticut River (p. 29)*, which also forms the state boundary with Vermont. This is the street that leads to *Montpelier (p. 69)*, the smallest state capital in the country. The town is the ideal place for hooking up with the scenic Route 100 *(it begins 40 km to the west and leads south)*. The country road runs along the eastern slopes of the *Green Mountains (p. 69)*, through villages such as *Warren* and *West Bridgewater*, from which a short hop takes you via Route 4 to *Woodstock (p. 73)*. Highly recommended. The area, heavy with history, is a Rockefeller possession and is cared for by the family. Similarly charming is *Newfane* in the south of Vermont, which you can reach via Route 30 if you leave Route 100 in *East Jamaica* travelling southeast. The lust green of the meadows and woods, along with the white frame houses set in the hilly landscape, are a perfect picture of New England. The stretch leads further to *Brattleboro (p. 63)*, the first settlement of Vermont Colony's founders.

The small town offers the opportunity to take a canoe or steamer down the Connecticut River. The 160 km back to Boston can be done via the I 91 and from Exit 27 eastwards on Route 2.

③ FOLLOWING THE LOBSTERS: THE ROUGH COAST OF MAINE

 From York Harbor to Acadia National Park, going shopping in Freeport and to the lobster pounds on the Atlantic. If you wish to enjoy the route and the meals, you'll need at least five days.

In the cold waters of the Atlantic along the rocky coast of northern New England marvellous sea creatures thrive: prawns, clams, crabs and above all lobster, which are to be had at the most reasonable prices at the lobster pounds. The following route with insider tips for a summer's feasting orgy follows Route 1 along the shores of Maine. The trip begins in the south of Maine, in *York Harbor (p. 83, 100 km north of Boston)*, where you should head for *Cape Neddick Lobster Pound (Shore Rd.)*. *Ogunquit (p. 82)*, an artists colony with a five-mile sand beach, follows further northwards. There you'll find lobster delicacies at *Barnacle Billy's Lobster Shack (Perkins Cove)* and at *Ogunquit Lobster Pound (Route 1)*. The next stop is *Kennebunkport (p. 81)*. On Ocean Avenue you'll find *Port Lobster Co.* and *Mabel's*. The trip to the north leads through *Freeport (p. 81)*, a shopping metropolis, which has been put on the map by the clothing manufacturer L.L.Bean *(open 24 hours)*. What's there? Outlet stores with American name-brand prod-

ucts. The next destination is *Boothbay Harbor (p. 78, in Wiscasset on Route 27 to the sea)*. The fishing village with the fjord-like harbour is proud to serve on the Atlantic with two restaurants – *Lobstermen's Co-Op* and *Cap'n Fish* – and on Commercial Street with one: *Ebb Tide*. *Pemaquid Point* with its famous lighthouse (one of 61 in Maine) is an ideal look-out point to enjoy the craggy coast *(in Newcastle turn on to Route 129 and 130)*.

Only with *Penobscot Bay* does the "true" Maine begin for purists: from then on it gets very lonesome. But those who turn back early miss sailing centres like *Camden (p. 79)*, *Rockport (p. 50)* and *Rockland (p. 22)*, where boats can be chartered. Two tips relating to lobster: the *Sail Loft* in Rockport harbour (oysters, too) and *Landings Restaurant* in the Rockland boat port. Further north turn off in *Ellsworth* at Route 3 to reach *Acadia National Park (p. 76)*, *Mount Desert Island, Bar Harbor (p. 78)* and *Bass Harbor (p. 78)*. There you'll find the glory of opulent summer residences built by well-to-do burghers of the 19th century, and sea food galore: for instance at *Beal's Lobster Pier (in the harbour)* in *Southwest Harbor (p. 78)* and in *Burning Tree (Route 3)* in *Otter Creek*. If your wish is to get back to Boston somewhat more quickly: you'll be there the soonest with the I 95. The distance is approx. 430 km. Recommended: along the way McDonald's has also got into the act, serving tasty *lobster rolls* for a mere $3.99 and not a penny more!

Practical information

The most important addresses and other information for your trip to New England

AMERICAN & BRITISH ENGLISH

Marco Polo travel guides are written in British English. In North America, certain terms and usages deviate from British usage. Some of the more frequently encountered examples are:
baggage for luggage, billion for thousand million, cab for taxi, car rental for car hire, drugstore for chemist's, fall for autumn, first floor for groundfloor, freeway/highway for motorway, gas(oline) for petrol, railroad for railway, restroom for toilet/lavatory, streetcar for tram, subway for underground/tube, toll-free numbers for freephone numbers, trailer for caravan, trunk for boot, vacation for holiday, wait staff for waiting staff (in restaurants etc.), zip code for postal code.

BANKS, MONEY & CREDIT CARDS

Banks in the US *(business hours generally Mon–Thurs 10 am–3 pm, Fri 10 am–5 pm, in many places Sat 10 am–12 am)* do not serve as money changers. They will, however, cash travellers' checks and will provide carriers of credit cards with cash. It is advisable to have a small amount of US currency on one's person upon arrival in order to pay the porters, taxi, bus and the like.

1 dollar = 100 cents. Bills exist in the following denominations 1, 2, 5, 10, 20, 100 dollars. Coins in the denominations: 1, 5, 10, 25, 50 cents. Other designations for the coins include: *penny* (1¢), *nickel* (5¢), *dime* (10¢), *quarter* (25¢), *buck* (1$). By far, the most popular means of payment is via the credit card. Travellers' checks are also accepted, e.g. from American Express *(in case of loss: Tel. 1/800/221 72 82).*

CAMPING

Information available from the state tourist offices. The most beautiful camping spots are in the *State Parks.* Reservations for 25 *national parks* accepted by the *National Park Service*: *Tel. 301/722 12 57; information on facilities and prices: www.nps.gov.*

CAR RENTAL

Rental cars are most reasonable when booked from one's home country. Should it happen that you're unable to deposit the vehicle at its original point of rental, horrendous secondary fees are to be reckoned with. Here it is more than advised to undertake a comparison of offers available. Whoever wishes to rent an auto in the US may make a reservation by telephone at no extra (telephone) charge:

Avis 1/800/331 12 12
Budget 1/800/527 07 00
Dollar 1/800/421 68 68
Hertz 1/800/654 31 31
National 1/800/328 45 67

Branch offices at airports in Boston and New York are located just off the arrival and departure terminals.

CLIMATE/WHEN TO GO

There's an old saying: if you don't like the weather in New England wait five minutes – it's sure to change. There are changeable days, to be sure, but by and large the seasons are well distinguishable from each other: summer in the coastal stretches are often hot and humid, inland pleasantly. The colourful autumn offers warm and sunny days (hovering around 20°C (68°F) into October), but chilly nights. In winter, snow cloaks New England from head to toe. Spring arrives relatively late. The highs and lows extend from steady below-zero temperatures in January and February to summer days when the thermometer actually reaches 30° (86°F).

CONSULATES

Boston:
British Consulate General (U/E-F5)
25th floor, Federal Reserve Plaza, 600 Atlantic Avenue, Boston MA
02210; Tel. 617/248 95 55; Fax 617/248 95 78

Canadian Consulate (U/A-B4)
Suite 400, Copley Plaza, Boston, MA 02216; Tel. 617/262 37 60

New York:
British Consulate General
845 Third Avenue, New York NY 10022; Tel. 212/745 02 00; Fax 212/754 30 62

Canadian Consulate
16th Floor, Exxon Bldg, 1251 Avenue of the America, New York NY 10020-1175

CUSTOMS

Plants, meat-products, fruit and sundry fresh groceries may not be brought to the US. On the positive side: 200 cigarettes or 50 cigars or 2 kg of tobacco as well as 1 litre of alcoholic beverages are allowed. In addition, gifts exceeding a value of $100 carry an import levy.

Into countries of the EU the following may be brought in free of customs duties: 1 litre of alcohol over 22%, 200 cigarettes or 100 cigarillos or 50 cigars or 250 gm tobacco, 50 gm perfume or 250 ml Eau de Cologne as well as other articles (excluding currency) not exceeding a total value of $170.

DRIVING

America's streets are classified (county routes, state highways, US highways, interstates). The numbers are found on all signposts. The speed limit in New Hampshire, Maine and Vermont: 65 mph (104 km/h) on interstates, 50 mph (80 km/h) on highways. In Connecticut, Massachusetts, Rhode Island and New York (Long Island): on most streets 55 mph (88 km/h).

At stop lights, it is permissible to make a right-hand turn. The so-called *3-way-* or *4-way stops*, that is an intersection with stop-signs in all four directions, the rule is that who first comes, first drives (when school buses stop at the right side of the road and turn on their blinkers, traffic *in both directions* must come to a halt).

There are no restaurants along the express ways. At most exits there are filling stations. Gallon *(1 gallon = 3,78 litre)* is the unit for petrol. In case of breakdowns, the AAA (American Automobile Association) offers help. Just to be on the safe side, carry your own auto club membership card with you.

EMERGENCIES

911 is the number for police and medical emergencies. It can be dialled from phone booths free of charge. The "emergency wards" of all hospitals are designated as such and obliged by law to treat patients not insured within the US. Though to gain admittance, one must be "delivered" via ambulance. "Walking wounded" (i.e. obviously non-critical arrivals transported by taxi or otherwise entering through the front entrance) will not be treated (gunshot wounds here being the exception). Note: international credit cards are useful in such a situation.

INFORMATION

Even if you don't happen to be one of those persons who plans a journey down to the very last detail, it is nevertheless still worth your while to inform yourself somewhat before setting out.

In Great Britain:
Yankee publishing Inc.
P.O. Box 520, Dublin, NH 03444; Tel. 603/563-81 11; www.NewEngland.com

In the USA:
Connecticut Department of Economic Development, Tourism Division
505 Hudson Street, Hartford, CT 06106; Tel. 860/270 80 21; www. tourism.state.ct.us

Maine Office of Tourism
59 State House Station, Augusta, ME 04333; Tel. 207/287 57 10; www.visitmaine.com

Massachusetts Office of Travel and Tourism
State transportation Bldg. 10 Park Plaza, Suite 4510, Boston MA 02116; Tel. 617/973 85 00; www.mass-vacation.com

New Hampshire Office of Travel and Tourism
172 Pembroke Rd., Concord, NH 03302-1856; Tel. 603/271 26 66; www.visit-newhampshire.com

Rhode Island Department of Economic Development, Tourism Division
1 W Exchange Street, Providence, RI 02903; Tel. 401/222 26 01; www.visitrhodeisland.com

Vermont Department of Tourism & Marketing
134 State Street, Montpelier, VT 05601; Tel. 802/828 32 36; www. travel-vermont.com

MEASURES & WEIGHTS

1 cm	0.39 inches
1 m	1.09 yards (3.28 feet)
1 km	0.62 miles
1 m²	1.20 sq yards
1 ha	2.47 acres
1 km²	0.39 sq miles
1 g	0.035 ounces
1 kg	2.21 pounds
1 British tonne	1016 kg
1 US ton	907 kg

1 litre is equivalent to 0.22 Imperial gallons and 0.26 US gallons

NUDISM

Public nude-bathing is strictly forbidden. Nudist beaches do exist – fenced off and in private hands.

PASSPORT & VISA

Only those planning to remain longer than 3 months are obliged to obtain a visa at home. On arrival a return ticket or proof of sufficient funds may in some cases be required (a credit card is sufficient). Passengers changing flights will handle all customs and passport formalities at the airport of initial arrival in the US.

POST & TELEPHONE

Post offices are open Mon–Fri 9 am–5 pm, many on Sat 9 am–12 am. Stamps can also be purchased in pharmacies or "drug stores". Postage: airmail to Europe (up to 20 g) 60¢, airmail postcards 50¢.
All telephone numbers in the US are 7-digit. For local calls only the number itself is necessary. For long-distance calls dial *1* first and then the 3-digit *area code.*

Locals calls from a telephone booth cost 25–30¢. Telephoning at reasonable prices are possible with a telephone card. Available for $5, 10, 20.

For all telephone difficulties there's always the *operator 0,* which will also accept *collect calls.* Free-of-charge numbers, with which one may reserve hotels, flights and rental vehicles, have the prefix *1-800.*

Prefix from the UK to the US: *001*; from the US to the UK: *001-44.* Prefix within the US: *001.*

PUBLIC TRANSPORT

The railway concern *Amtrak* joins New York and Boston. Information – also with regard to rail passes allowing one to travel at a reduced rate – at Amtrak offices: direct in the US (Tel. 1-800-USA-RAIL) and under http://www.amtrak.com in the Internet or via your local travel agency.

Greyhound links numerous cities with overland bus routes. Information at all travel agencies.

TELEVISION & RADIO

Via UHF or satellite TV you can receive more than 30 channels, among them ABC, CBS and NBC. In addition: CNN – Cable News Network (round-the-clock news reports), ESPN (24 hour sport), Weather Channel (24 hour weather reports), MTV (24 hours of pop-videos).

TIME ZONES

Eastern Standard Time: daylight saving time (+1hr): the first Sunday in April until the last Sunday in October.

TIPPING

In the prices restaurants display on their menus, no consideration is made for the service personal. As consequence, the 15% tip recommended to patrons assumes, for this sector of the working populace, a bigger-than-life dimension. B.N., in America your generosity goes towards your waiter's or waitress's sustenance!

TOILETS

Public conveniences are few and far between. Petrol stations, supermarkets, restaurants and hotels may offer relief.

VOLTAGE

110 Volt/60 Hertz. Smaller devices at this voltage as well, but one should have an adapter equipped with plugs matching US sockets.

YOUTH HOSTELS

YMCA (men), YWCA (women). Bed in the American Youth Hostels (AYH) must be reserved in advance. Information: *Hostelling International Handbook, Vol. 2.*

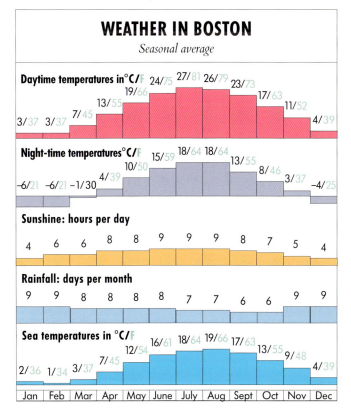

WEATHER IN BOSTON
Seasonal average

Daytime temperatures in °C/F
3/37 3/37 7/45 13/55 19/66 24/75 27/81 26/79 23/73 17/63 11/52 4/39

Night-time temperatures °C/F
-6/21 -6/21 -1/30 4/39 10/50 15/59 18/64 18/64 13/55 8/46 3/37 -4/25

Sunshine: hours per day
4 6 6 8 8 9 9 9 8 7 5 4

Rainfall: days per month
9 9 8 8 8 8 7 7 6 6 9 9

Sea temperatures in °C/F
2/36 1/34 3/37 7/45 12/54 16/61 18/64 19/66 17/63 13/55 9/48 4/39

| Jan | Feb | Mar | Apr | May | June | July | Aug | Sept | Oct | Nov | Dec |

Do's and don'ts

Where you have to be careful in order that your journey is a complete success

Jet lag

Don't give yourself over to jet-lag fatigue when you arrive in the US. The time shift of five hours from Great Britain to the American east coast requires three days for compensation. Following arrival (mostly after-noons) it is recommended to battle that old tired feeling or take, at most, a 2-hour nap. Sea-soned travellers fight jet lag, in-tensified through the dry air conditioning inside the plane, by drinking lots of mineral water.

Criminality

Taking a drive through the unfa-miliar streets or neighbourhoods of large cities like Boston, Hart-ford, New Haven, Bridgeport or Providence is simply mad. As much as the New England coun-tryside offers a well-tended ap-pearance, yet that impression should not inspire you to care-lessness – crime in these me-tropoles is, like everywhere else in the US extremely high. Tourists are incidentally pre-ferred victims of muggings. Your money or your life! That's the threat during many rob-beries, even today. If it ever happens to you, do not resist in any way! Whoever is threaten-ing you is likely to apply any kind of violence necessary. The best thing to do is to surrender your money, which will pro-bably save you from anything worse.

Stings, bites, jabs

Don't take the charm of the New England forests wrongly! As much as they may recall European woods, all the less can the former be compared with the latter. Ticks, which carry and transmit the nasty Lyme Disease (possible consequence: meningitis), rabid racoons and ever-present *(poison ivy)* are among the constant dangers. Warm weather brings veritable black clouds of hungry mosqui-toes. Creams and lotions allevi-ate their ferocity. Recom-mended first and foremost against other unpleasantness are hats, scarves and button-up clothing.

Revving it up

You're waiting at a red light, and the person in the car next to you lets his engine roar, revving it up – an invitation to partake in a small race once the light turns green. Let him race onward, but without you. He has a souped-up motor, you don't. He'll just keep racing away from the police. They'll stop you instead.

Road Atlas of New England

*Please refer to the back cover for an overview
of this Road Atlas*

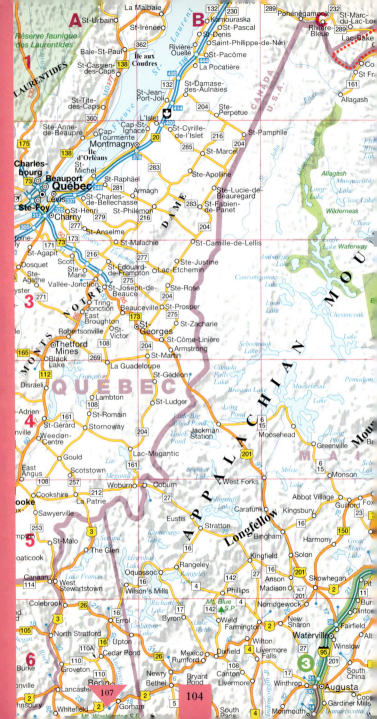

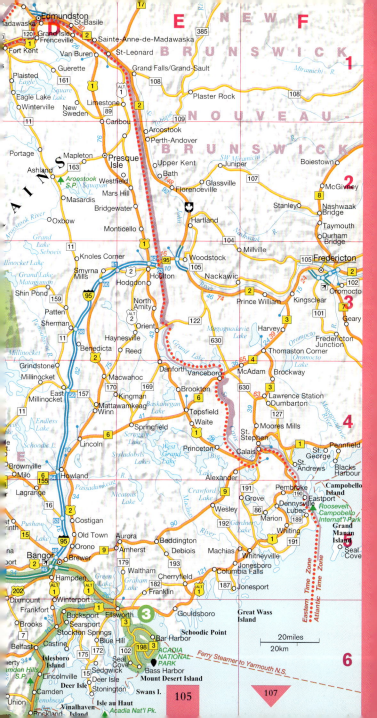

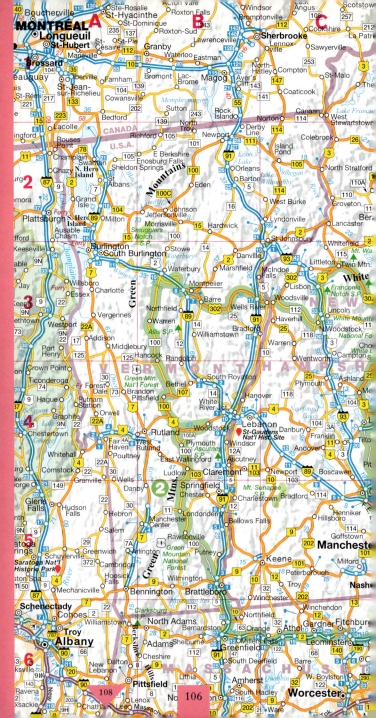

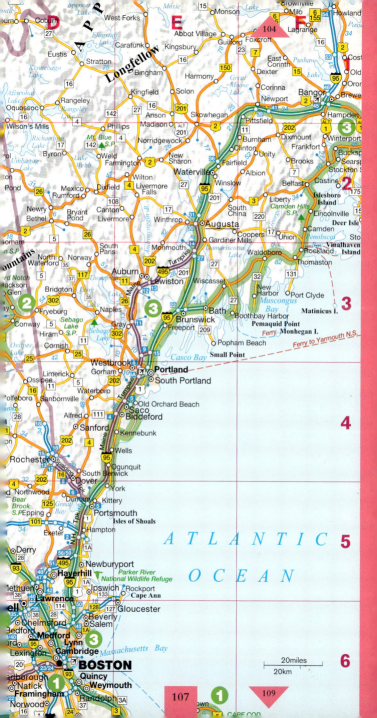

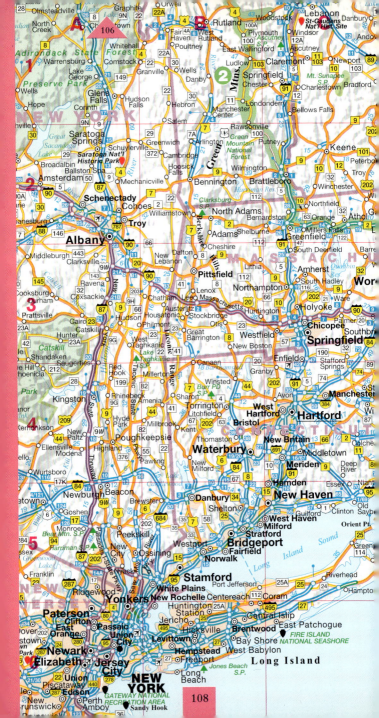

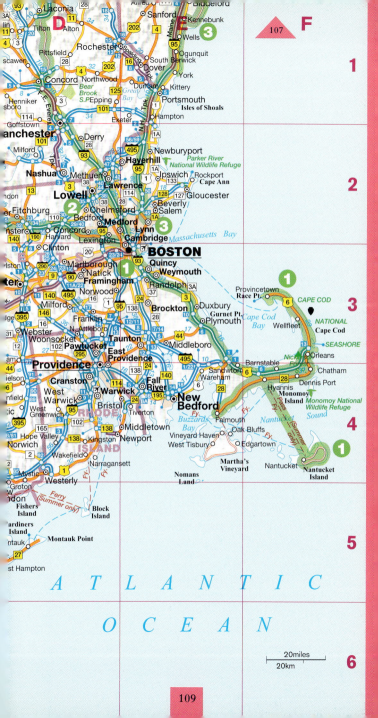

German	Symbol	English
Gebührenfreie Autobahn mit Anschlußstelle und Nummer	272	Controlled access highway with interchange and exit number
Gebührenpflichtige Autobahn		Controlled access toll highway
Hauptverbindungsstraße		Principal through highway
Nebenstraße		Other through highway
Interstate Highway	20	Interstate highway
US-Highway	98 68	US highway
Trans-Kanada-Highway		Trans-Canada highway
Bundesstaat- oder Provinzhighway	40 75	State or provincial highway
Entfernung (Meilen/Kilometer)	25 40	Distance (Miles/Kilometres)
Internationale Grenze		International boundary
Provinz- oder Bundesstaatsgrenze		Provincial, territorial or state boundary
Auto-, Personenfähre		Car-, passenger ferry
Zeitzonengrenze		Time zone boundary
National-, Bundesstaat-, Provinzpark		National/state/provincial Park
Erholungs- oder Schutzgebiet		Recreational area or reserve
US Nationalpark		US National Park
Sehenswürdigkeit unter Nationalparkverwaltung		US National Park Service
Kanadischer Nationalpark		Parks Canada
US Bundesforstverwaltung		US Forest Service
Wichtiges Naturschutzgebiet		Major National Wildlife Refuge
Ausgewählter Staats-/Provinzpark		Selected state/provincial park
Sehenswürdigkeit		Point of interest
Wichtiger Flughafen		Major airport
Stadtgebiet		Built-up area
Städte und Ortschaften	ATLANTA● Pittsburgh◉ Pensacola◎ Mayfield○	Populated centres
(Schrift und Signatur abhängig von Einwohnerzahl)		(Type size and dot indicative of population)
Hauptstadt	WASHINGTON	National capital
Bundesstaats-/Provinzhauptstadt	RICHMOND	State/provincial/territorial capital

20 miles
20 km

INDEX

This index lists all the main places and sights mentioned in this guide.
Numbers in bold indicate a main entry, italics a photograph.

Places

Bar Harbor 22, **78**
Barnstable 48
Bass Harbor 78
Bennington 62
Boothbay Harbor 22, **78**
Boston 6, *14*, 21, 22, 23,
  38, 39, **40**, *41*, *43*
Brattleboro 23, **63**
Bretton Woods 72
Brewster 48
Bridgehampton 23, **86**
Burlington 22, **64**, 65
Cambridge/Harvard *10*, 23, **46**
Camden 79
Chatham 47
Chilmark 52
Concord 21, **65**
Cornwall 28
East Hampton 23, **87**
Edgartown 52
Essex 29
Falmouth 47
Farmington 22
Freeport 81
Gay Head 52
Gloucester 22, **50**
Great Barrington 51
Greenville 81
Hancock 22
Hanover 66
Hartford 6, **29**, *30*, *31*
Harwich 23
Hyannis 47, 53
Kennebunkport 81
Killington 67
Lakeville/Salisbury 30
Lancaster 73
Lenox 22, **51**
Litchfield 31
Manchester NH 68
Manchester VT 68
Marblehead 59
Marlboro 63
Montauk 89
Montpelier 69
Mystic 32, *33*
Narragansett 34
New Bedford 53, **56**
New Haven 23, **34**
New Marlborough 51
Newport 22, 23, **34**, *35*
North Conway 72
North Fork Long Island 91
Northeast Harbor 78
Oak Bluffs 52
Ogunquit 82
Old Lyme 37
Old Wethersfield 30
Pittsfield 56
Plymouth 6, 23, **57**, *58*
Portland 82
Portsmouth 6, 22, **69**, *70*
Providence 6, **37**
Provincetown 47, **48**
Rockland 22
Rockport 50
Sag Harbor 91
St Johnsbury 70
Salem 22, **58**
Salisbury/Lakeville 30
Sandwich 48
Seal Harbor 78
Sheffield 51
South Egremont 51
Southampton *84*, 92
Southfield 51

Southwest Harbor 78
Stonington **37**, 80
Stowe 21, **71**
Sturbridge 59
Sugarbush 23
Tanglewood/Lenox 51
Tenants Harbor 80
Uncasville 36
Vineyard Haven 52
Wellfleet 48
West Tisbury 52
Woods Hole **47**, 53
Woodstock 73
Yale/New Haven 22, **34**
Yarmouthport 48
York 83

Sights, museums, excursions

Astor's Beechwood, the
  Newport 35
Beinecke Rare Book Library,
  Yale/New Haven 34
Bennington Museum 63
Block Island
  Historical Society 27
Boothbay Railway Village,
  Boothbay 78
Boston Harbor Cruises, Boston 42
Boston Symphony Orchestra,
  Tanglewood 51
Boston Tea Party Ship and
  Museum, Boston 42
Bowen's Wharf, Newport 35
Canterbury Shaker Village 65
Computer Museum, Boston 42
Connecticut Valley Railroad 29
Currier Gallery of Art,
  Manchester NH 68
Floating Bridge, Montpelier 69
Foxwoods Casino, Ledyard 6, **36**
Freedom Trail, Boston 42
Gilded Age Cottages, Lenox 51
Gilded Age Newport 35
Gilette Castle State Park,
  Hadlyme 29
Goodspeed Opera House,
  East Haddam 29
Hammersmith Farm,
  Fort Adams 35
Hancock Shaker Village,
  Pittsfield 57
Harvard University *10*, 46
Historic Deerfield,
  Cape Cod 50
House of the Seven Gables,
  Salem 59
Isabella Stewart Gardner Museum,
  Boston 42
John F. Kennedy Library
  and Museum, Boston 43
Mark Twain House
  (Nook Farm), Hartford 30
Museum of Fine Arts, Boston 43
Mystic Marinelife Aquarium 32
Mystic Seaport Museum 33
New England Aquarium,
  Boston 42
New England Maple Museum,
  Pittsford 68
Norman Rockwell Museum,
  Lenox 52
Old Sturbridge Village 21, **59**
Parrish Art Museum,
  Southampton 92
Peabody and Essex Museum,
  Salem 59

Pilgrim Hall Museum,
  Plymouth 58
Plimouth Plantation,
  Plymouth 58
Portland Museum of Art 83
Shelburne Museum,
  Burlington 64
Tennis Hall of Fame, Newport 36
Wadsworth Atheneum, Hartford 30
Whaling Museum, Nantucket 54
Whaling Museum, Sag Harbor 91
Yale Center for British Art 34
Yale University Art Gallery 34
York Historical Society 83

Islands, natural monuments, beaches

Acadia National Park 13, **76**
Baxter State Park 82
Berkshire Mountains 13, **51**
Block Island 27
Cape Cod 40, **46**
Chappaquiddick Island 52
Charlestown Beachway,
  State Park 34
Chebeague Island 83
Connecticut River, Valley of the *24*, 29
Deer Isle 80
East Beach, Chappaquiddick
  Island 54
East Beach, Charlestown 34
Green Mountain Flyer,
  Manchester VT 69
Hammonasset Beach State Park,
  Madison 37
Isle au Haut 77
Isles of Shoals 70
Islesboro Island 80
Kancamagus Highway 72
Lake Champlain 64
Lake Sunapee 67
Lake Waramaug 32
Lake Winnipesaukee 66
Madaket Beach, Nantucket 56
Main Beach, East Hampton 87
Martha's Vineyard 52, *53*
Matunuck Beach 34
Matunuck State Beach 34
Monhegan Island 79
Moonstone Beach,
  Charlestown 34
Moosehead Lake 81
Mount Washington 71
Nantucket 54, *55*
National Wildlife Refuge
  Monomoy Island 48, **49**
New Bedford
  Whaling Museum 56
North Beach Island,
  Cape Cod 48
Penobscot Bay 79, 80
Quechee Gorge 73
Roger W. Wheeler Memorial
  Beach, Point Judith 34
Route 127 A 50
Roy Carpenter's Beach,
  Matunuck 34
Shelter Island 92
Siasconset Beach, Nantucket 56
South Beach,
  Chappaquiddick Island 54
South Beach Island, Cape Cod 48
South County Atlantic
  Beach Park, Watch Hill 34
Surfside Beach, Nantucket 56
Wale Watching 50
White Mountains 13, **71**, *72*

What do you get for your money?

The dollar, the world's standard currency, has been rising for some time. And with that, currency exchange rates are not quite as favourable as they once were, yet visitors can still expect to get a lot for their money. That begins with air fares and holds true for car rentals, incidentally in New England the preferred mode of transportation. A compact *(subcompact or economy car)* costs – with no restrictions regarding mileage – seldom more than $200 per week. Gas prices can fluctuate wildly, but expect to pay between 40 and 60 cents per litre.

Other prices for comparison's sake: coffee in a coffee shop costs 75 cent a cup. A lobster roll, that's a bread roll with fresh lobster salad, costs in Maine's coastal resort area $ 10. Ben & Jerry's Ice Cream from Vermont (try: the variety *Health Bar Crunch)* is $1.75 per scoop. A half-day voyage by ship to Stellwagen Banke, the feeding grounds of the whales, will cost you from Gloucester $25, the bike on Long Island $20 per day. Ten of the summer palaces of Vanderbilt & Co. can be viewed in

Newport for $47. The trip to Mount Washington costs with the oldest mountain train in the world costs $44; on foot, however, as mentioned above, it's completely free of charge!

US$	£	Can$
1	0.61	1.44
2	1.22	2.87
3	1.83	4.31
4	2.44	5.74
5	3.05	7.18
10	6.10	14.36
20	12.21	28.71
30	18.31	43.07
40	24.41	57.43
50	30.52	71.79
60	36.62	86.14
70	42.72	100.50
80	48.82	114.86
90	54.93	129.22
100	61.03	143.57
200	122.06	287.15
300	183.09	430.72
400	244.12	574.29
500	305.15	717.87
750	457.73	1,076.80
1,000	610.30	1,435.73